In Blue Creek Cañon

(Anna Chapin Ray)

CONTENTS

CHAPTER I.

A COUNCIL ON SKATES.

A strong southeast wind was blowing up the cañon and driving before it the dense yellow smoke which rolled up from the great red chimneys of the smelter. To the east and west of the town, the mountains rose abruptly, their steep sides bare or covered with patches of yellow pine. At the north, the cañon closed in to form a narrow gorge between the mountains; but towards the south it opened out into a broad valley, through which the swiftly rushing creek twisted and turned along its willow-bordered bed. A half mile below the town the creek suddenly broadened into a little lake that was now frozen over, forming a sheet of dazzling ice, upon which a quartette of boys and girls were darting about on skates.

"Ugh!" gasped one of the boys, as a sudden gust of wind, coming straight from the east, brought the stifling cloud in their direction; "I'm glad I'm not up in town this afternoon. It's getting ready for a storm, I think, from the way the smoke comes down; and they must be catching it all, up there."

"Oh, dear!" sighed the girl with whom he was skating; "if it storms 'twill be sure to be more snow, and spoil the ice. It's too bad, for we get so little skating out here, and it's almost time to go home now. Just see how low the sun is getting!"

"Never mind, Marjorie," said the boy, as he paused to breathe on his cold fingers; then held out his hand to her once more. "We'll have one more go across the pond, anyway, for there's no knowing when we'll have another chance. You take Allie, Ned, and we'll race you, two and two, over to that largest stump. Come on, and get into line. One! two! *three!*"

Away they flew, the bright blades of their skates flashing in the long slanting rays of the late afternoon sun, and their eyes and cheeks glowing with the cold air and rapid exercise. Marjorie and her attendant knight were the first to reach the goal, and turned, panting, to face the others as they came up to them.

"That was just fine!" exclaimed Allie's companion, as he dropped her hand and spun around in a narrow circle which sent the chips of ice flying from under his heel. "Don't let's go home just yet, 't won't be dark for an hour anyway, and we can go up in fifteen minutes. I'll race you over to the other side and back again, Howard, while the girls are getting their breath."

"You don't mind being left, Allie?" And the taller boy glanced at the girls.

"All right, just for once," said Allie; "then we really ought to go up, Howard; mamma wants us to be home in good season to-night, for dinner is going to be early, so papa can get the train down."

"Is your father going away again?" asked Marjorie, as the girls skated idly to and fro, waiting for the boys to join them. "I thought he came in from camp only this morning."

"So he did," answered her friend, burying her small nose in her muff for a moment, as she faced the cutting wind. "He's only going down to Pocatello to-night, and out on the main line a little ways, to meet Charlie MacGregor, our cousin that's coming."

"Yes," nodded Marjorie, in acquiescence; "I remember now; I'd forgotten he was coming so soon. What fun you'll have with him, Allie! I wish I had a brother, or cousin, or something."

"Perhaps I shall wish I didn't have both," said Allie, laughing. "I don't know how he and Howard will get on. I think Howard doesn't want him much; but I'd just as soon he'd be here."

"What's he like?" queried Marjorie curiously.

"I haven't much idea; I've never seen him," said Allie. "Papa saw him when he was east last summer, and we have a picture of him taken ever so long ago."

"Who's that--Charlie MacGregor?" asked Howard, skating up to them at that moment. "He's not much to look at, Marjorie, if his picture's any good. He has a pug nose and wears giglamps, and I've a suspicion that he's a fearful dude. He'll be a tenderfoot, of course, but he'll get over that; but if he's a dude, we boys will make it lively for him."

"Howard, you sha'n't!" remonstrated his sister, loyally coming to the defence of their unknown cousin. "It must be horrid for him to lose all his friends and have to be sent out here to relations he doesn't know nor care anything about, just like a barrel of flour." Allie's metaphors were becoming mixed; but she never heeded that, as she went on proudly: "And besides, we're MacGregors as much as he is, and mamma says that no MacGregor was ever rude to a cousin, or to anybody in trouble."

"Good for you, Allie!" shouted the younger boy, as he stopped in the middle of a figure eight to applaud her words. "You're in the right of it; but you needn't think you'll ever keep Howard in order. How old is this lad, anyhow?"

"Half way between Howard and me," replied Allie, as they started to skate slowly up the creek towards home, and Howard and Marjorie dropped a little in the rear. "He was thirteen last summer, and papa says he's a real, true musician. He'll bring his own piano with him; but I don't know where he'll find room to put it, for our house is full as can be, now. Then he sings, too,--at least, he used to,--in a boy choir. Haven't you seen his picture, Ned? It's homely, but it looks as if he might not be so bad."

"Where's he coming from?" asked Ned.

"New York. He's lived there always; but, you know, his father died two years ago, and his mother last month. He hasn't any relations but just us, so he is to live here for a while. You and Howard will stand by him, won't you, Ned?" she added persuasively, laying her mittened hand on his. "I'm afraid the other boys will run on him and make fun of him. Don't tell Howard I said so, but I don't expect to like him much myself, only I'm sort of sorry for him; and then he's our cousin, so I suppose we must make sure he has a good time."

"I won't be hard on him, Allie," her companion answered her, laughing a little at the unwonted seriousness of her tone; "as long as he doesn't put on airs and talk big about New York and 'the way _we_ do East,' and all that poppycock, I'll stand by him. But if he's coming out here to show us how to do it, the sooner it's taken out of him the better."

"Wait till the train comes in, day after to-morrow morning, Ned," said Howard, as, with a few quick strokes, he and Marjorie overtook them once more. "We'll take a look at him and see what he's like, before we make too many promises. Now, then, ma'am," he added, as he and Marjorie paused at a great stone on the bank of the creek; "if you'll be good enough to sit down, I'll have your skates off instanter."

Marjorie laughed, as she dropped down on the stone and put one little foot on Howard's knee, while Ned performed a similar service for Allie.

"I'm crazy to see your cousin, Allie," she said. "I know he's going to be great fun, only I'm afraid he'll think we are hopeless tomboys. Probably he's been used to girls that sit in the parlor and sew embroidery, instead of skating and riding bronchos bareback, and playing hare and hounds with the boys."

"Don't care if he has!" And Allie made a little grimace of defiance as she scrambled to her feet. "I'm not going to give up all my good times and take to fancy work, when it's as much as I can do to sew on my own buttons. He can stay in the house, and sing songs and sew patchwork all day long, if he wants to, but I'm not going to give up all my frolics; need I, boys?" she concluded, in a mutinous outburst, quite at variance with her recent plea for their expected guest.

Howard laughed teasingly.

"Catch Allie turning the fine young lady! If you shut her up in a parlor, she'd jump over the chairs and play tag with herself around the table; and Marjorie is about as bad."

"Perhaps I am," she assented placidly; "but you boys could never get along without us. I've heard you say, over and over again, that we can catch a ball as well as half the boys in town, and I can outrun you any day. Want to try?"

"Not much," returned Howard, laughing, though there rankled in his mind the memory of recent races in which he had not been the winner. "You only beat me because you've been used to this air longer than I have. Besides, it would hurry us home too much, and I've an idea that this may be the last time that we four chums will be off together, for one while. I shall have to trot round with that fellow, for the next week, and show him the ways of the country, so he won't make too great a jay of himself. But, I say, if it doesn't storm to-morrow, we'll come down here again in the afternoon, and have an hour or two on the ice before it's spoiled."

With their skates strapped together and slung over their shoulders, their collars turned up around their ears, and their hands plunged deep into pockets and muffs, they turned northward along the bank of the creek for a short distance, and then struck off across the level, open ground till they came into one of the streets of the little town, which they followed until they reached the main business street. There they parted, Ned and Marjorie turning to the west, while Howard and Allie kept straight on towards the north, and finally stopped at a small brick house, a low, one-story affair, yet much more elaborate than the average dwelling of the town, where the architecture was largely of the log-house species, though often covered with a layer of boards to disguise the primitive nature of the materials.

The front door opened directly into the little parlor, and into this cosy room Howard and Allie plunged, laughing and breathless after their quick walk in the cold. A bright-faced little woman sat sewing by the front window, holding up her work to catch the last fading light, and a rosy boy, two years old, was tumbling about on the carpet, rolling over and over the great dog, who was dozing as peacefully as if such demonstrations were quite to his liking.

"Hullo, mammy! Hullo, Vic! Dinner ready?" exclaimed Howard, casting his skates into the nearest chair, and moving up to the stove to warm his chilled fingers.

"How was the skating?" asked his mother, looking up from her work to smile at Allie, as she pulled off her coat and hat, and then caught up the child from the floor.

"Fine; but we're 'most starved--at least, I am," returned Howard, as he wriggled himself out of his coat and handed it to Allie, who received it quite as a matter of course, and went away to hang it in its usual place.

"Well, dinner is all ready, and papa will be here in a minute; so you can go and tell Janey to take it up. Do you know," she added, with a laugh which took all the sting from the reproof; "I think it is time my boy learned to take his sister's coat for her, instead of expecting her to wait on him."

"All right," answered Howard, by no means abashed by the rebuke. "Here, sis, if you'll just bring back your coat and put it on again, I'll see what can be done about it." And he bent over to stroke his mother's hair with a boyish affection which filled her heart with gratitude for having such a son, even while it sent her off to her toilet table to repair the damages which his fingers had wrought. Then he marched out to the kitchen to tease Janey, until she threatened to pour the soup over his favorite pudding, unless he left her to take up the dinner in peace.

Mr. Burnam, Howard's father, was a successful civil engineer, who, in the line of his professional life, had been ordered up and down the West according to the demands of the great railroad corporation by whom he was employed. The life of a locating engineer is much like that of the soldier, in its need for strict obedience to orders, and for eighteen years Mr. Burnam had been stationed, now here, now there,--on the rolling prairies of Iowa, in the Dakota bad lands, in the alkali deserts of Wyoming, and among the cañons and passes of the Colorado Rockies. Six months before this time he had been ordered to western Montana, to lay out a possible railway across the mountains, which should give the Pacific-coast cities a more direct connection with their eastern neighbors. The survey for this line would occupy him for a year or more, and in order to have his family near him during this time, he had made his headquarters in the little mining camp, which the first prospectors along the cañon, some four years before, had christened "Blue Creek," from the clear, bright waters of the mountain stream. Here he established his family in the most comfortable house that the town afforded, and here he had his office, which served as headquarters for his corps of men, whenever they came in town for a few days. By virtue of his position as chief of the party, Mr. Burnam often spent weeks at a time at home, working up his estimates and maps, and only driving out to camp now and then, for a day or two, to see that all was well in his absence. Then, just as his family were settling down to the full enjoyment of his society, he would be sent for, to oversee some difficult bit of work, and Mrs. Burnam and Allie would be left to the protection of Howard, and of Ben, the great Siberian bloodhound, who was as gentle as a kitten until molested, when all his old savage instincts sprang into life.

One of the early graduates from Cornell, Mr. Burnam had gone West when a mere boy, fresh from college; and now, at forty, he had made himself a brilliant reputation in his profession. The chief, as they called him, was adored by all his men, who knew, from long experience, that however great the danger and hardship might be, he was always ready to share it with them, and that he made it a part of his creed never to ask a subordinate to take a risk which he himself would shun. Quick-tempered and outspoken in the presence of any suspicion of shirking or deceit, he was yet a just, honorable man in dealing with his "boys," who loved and respected him accordingly. At home, he was a different man; for he threw aside his professional dignity, to tease his wife, or romp with his children, lavishing upon them all the love of which his great, generous nature was capable.

For the sake of her husband, Mrs. Burnam had willingly cut herself adrift from her family and friends in New York, and for sixteen years she had patiently followed him here and there through the West; now living in camp for a summer, now boarding at tiny country hotels, in order to be within driving distance of his party; now left for months at a time in the busy solitude of a great city hotel, while Mr. Burnam was far away in unexplored forests, and often, as now, settled near him for a few months of housekeeping which should give her children at least a slight knowledge of home life and its charms.

Two years after her marriage, a little son had come to her, and, soon after that, a daughter had helped to fill out the family circle. It seemed to Mrs. Burnam but a few months since then; but Howard was fourteen now, and Allie twelve, while, two years before this time, a third child had come to brighten the home with his baby prattle and pranks. For weeks, his name had been a subject of almost constant discussion, until, one day, Howard had solved the problem in a most unexpected fashion.

"I'll tell you what," he said suddenly; "name him Victor, for my new bicycle." And the name was decided upon accordingly.

Howard, himself, was a worthy son of the handsome, brown-bearded man whom he called papa. Tall, slender, and yellow haired, he was as bonnie a laddie as ever filled a mother's heart with pride; a healthy, happy boy, affectionate and generous, and full of a rollicking fun which made him at once the delight and terror of his sister, who never knew in what direction his next outbreak would come. In spite of his merciless teasing, the brother and sister were close friends and constantly together. Girls were scarce in the town, and Allie and her one friend, Marjorie Fisher, would have been largely left to their own devices, had it not been for Howard and Ned Everett, through whose influence they were received on equal terms among the boys, and had a share in most of their good times. It was no uncommon thing to hear them speak of "Allie and Marjorie and the other boys," and neither Mrs. Burnam nor Mrs. Fisher felt any desire to have it otherwise. They were too sensible mothers to force their little daughters towards womanhood, and much preferred the tone of free-and-easy companionship to the childish flirtations so commonly indulged in. They could trust to their influence over their children to keep them gentle and womanly, and the boys were all gentlemen, largely sons of Eastern men whom business had brought to the town. So the girls walked and rode, skated and romped with the lads, unconsciously teaching them many a pretty lesson in chivalry, while in return the boys gave them a training which made them enduring and courageous, and hardy as a pair of little Indians. For six months, this had been their life, and by this time there had formed one well-recognized set whose members were constantly together, and, though they mingled more or less with the other young people, yet kept themselves distinct from their companions. Four of this number were the little group of skaters, the fifth was Ned's younger brother, Grant, who was usually the central figure in their frolics.

The one other member of the Burnam household, who is as yet in the background, deserves at least a passing remark. This was Janey, the young negro maid who ruled their kitchen. What had ever brought her from the warm South into the midst of Rocky Mountain snows, it would be hard to tell; but, two months before, she had answered to Mrs. Burnam's advertisement for a servant, and was promptly installed in her kitchen, where she convulsed the family with her pranks, and averted many a well-merited lecture by some sudden, artless remark, which sent Mrs. Burnam hurrying out of the room, in search of a corner where she could laugh unseen. Surely, since the days of Topsy, the immortal, there was never such an imp as Janey. Mrs. Burnam declared that she was as good as a tonic, and Mr. Burnam made no secret of his enjoyment of her antics, which were always as original as they were unexpected.

"My name's Edmonia Jackson," she had said, in answer to Mrs. Burnam's question; "but dey mos'ly calls me Janey. But laws, Mis', ef you 'll on'y let me stay yere, you all can call me what you want. Names is nothin', but I don' want to work in one o' them log-cabins; they 's too much like what our po' w'ites lives in. Give me brick or nothin'!"

CHAPTER II.

TO WELCOME THE COMING GUEST.

"Only ten minutes more!" said Allie, excitedly prancing up and down the platform. "I do so hope the train won't be late."

"Allie's getting in a hurry to see the cousin," remarked Grant Everett teasingly. "You and Howard'll have to step out of the way when he comes, Ned. You needn't think you're going to stand any chance against this new attraction."

"Maybe so," said Howard scornfully, while he flattened his nose against the ticket-office window, in a vain endeavor to see the clock. "Girls always like a new face, and Allie's just like all the rest of them."

"No," said Allie judicially, as she pulled the collar of her fur jacket more closely about her ears. "Of course I like you boys best, but I'm sort of curious about Charlie, as long as he's going to live with us for a year or so. If he's nice, it will be like having another brother; but if he's horrid, it will spoil all our good times. It's a very dependable circumstance, as Janey says, that's all."

It was the second morning after their skating party, and Howard, Allie, and the two Everett boys were pacing up and down the platform, while they waited for the coming of the train which should bring them their new companion. They formed an attractive little group as they moved to and fro, talking and laughing, or pausing now and again to turn and gaze down the track, which stretched far away before them in two shining rows of steel. With the instinct of the true hostess, Allie had arrayed herself in her state and festival suit, and sallied forth to meet her father and cousin, and extend to their guest a prompt welcome to his new home. Half-way to the station she was surprised at being overtaken by the three boys, who came rushing after her, shouting her name as they ran.

"'Where are you going, my pretty maid?'" panted Ned, dropping into step at one side, while Howard took the other, and Grant capered along the sidewalk in front of them, now backwards, now sideways, and now forwards, as the conversation demanded his entire attention, or became uninteresting once more.

"'I'm going to meet Cousin Charlie, she said,'" answered Allie, laughing.

"So that's the why of all these fine feathers," commented Ned; while Howard added,--

"All right; we'll go with you."

"But I thought you just told mamma that you wouldn't go, anyway," responded Allie, astonished at this sudden change of plan.

"Well, I'm here," answered Howard calmly. "I'm not going to welcome him with open arms, though; and you needn't think I am. We fellows are just going to take a look at him on the sly, and then we can tell better how to treat him."

"But, Howard, you mustn't; he'll see you," remonstrated Allie, scandalized at the suggestion. "If papa knows it he won't like it a bit."

"Oh, that's all right, Allie," said Ned reassuringly. "All we 're going to do is to hide behind that pile of freight boxes over there, and get a good look at him without his knowing it. Then we'll light out for home, and Howard will be there ahead of you, see if he isn't; so, if you don't give it away, there'll be no harm done."

"Unless you tell of it yourselves," said Allie doubtfully. "I don't half like it; and if Howard won't help meet him, he ought to keep clear out of the way. But there's one thing about it, boys, you must, you really must, stop talking so much slang. It's bad enough with us girls, and I'm getting to use it as much as you do; but you'll scare Charlie to pieces if you talk so much of it."

"Does our right worshipful brother maintain himself in his usual health and spirits?--is that the style, Allie?" asked Howard, as he took off his cap with a flourish, and bowed low before some imaginary personage.

"I caught Allie studying the dictionary, yesterday morning," said Grant, turning to face them once more. "She had a piece of paper in her lap, with concatenation and peripatetic and nostalgia written on it, and I supposed she was studying her spelling lesson, but now I see,--she was just making up a sentence to say to him. Speak up loud, Allie, so we can hear."

"You'd better stay here and listen," said Allie. "But there's the train, see, just coming round the curve down the cañon. Off with you, if you really are going to be so silly!"

The boys whirled around hastily, to assure themselves that it was no false alarm; then they left her to wait alone, while they settled themselves behind a pile of great wooden boxes which half filled the upper end of the platform. Allie watched them arrange themselves at their ease; then, when they were quite hidden from view, she turned back to look at the train as it rushed up the valley towards her, sending along the rails before it a fierce throbbing which kept time to her own leaping pulse.

In spite of her light talk and laughter, Allie was conscious of a keen sense of excitement, as she stood waiting to receive her cousin. He was the only child of Mrs. Burnam's only brother; and now, at thirteen, he was left alone in the world, doubly orphaned, and with no near relatives save this one aunt, to whose care his dying mother had intrusted her boy. All that Allie knew had only served to interest her in the young stranger; his love for music and his unusual talent for it, his former life spent in a luxurious city home, even his present loneliness had touched her girlish heart with pity, and made her resolve to render his new life pleasant to him, in spite of the possible teasing he might have to undergo from the boys. And then, while she was determined to become his champion at any cost, there was always the delightful possibility that he might be a pleasant addition to their little circle, and contribute his share to the frolics which were continually taking place at either the Burnams' or the Everetts'. Far into the hours of the previous night she had lain awake, picturing her cousin as he would probably appear to them, and going over and over in her own mind the details of their first meeting. She was sorry that he had lost his mother; but she found herself fervently hoping that he would not be so very dismal, and even that he might laugh a little occasionally, when anything particularly amusing should occur.

"Well, daught, how goes it?" And Allie found herself in her father's arms, and then released, as Mr. Burnam added, "Here, Charlie, this is your Cousin Alice."

With a sudden shyness, Allie put her hand into the one before her, as she glanced up at the boyish face which was looking down into her own. Something she read there, in the half-anxious expression of the brown eyes, made her forget her more formal salutation, and say cordially,--

"Are you the new brother that's come to live at our house? It's going to be splendid to have you there." And with a little confiding, sisterly gesture, she pulled his hand through her arm, in an unspoken welcome which was inexpressibly grateful to the lad, tired with his three thousand miles of lonely journeying, and dreading to meet these strange cousins into whose home life he had been so abruptly forced. Now, as he looked at Allie's slight, girlish figure, and at her bright, happy face which not even her irregular features could render plain, he felt a sudden sense of relief, and secretly wished that all the family might be as attractive as his genial uncle and the pleasant cousin who had given him so sisterly a greeting.

"Come," she added, as her father beckoned to them; "we'll go over and get into that carriage, while papa hunts up your trunks." And she led the way across the platform with an apparent unconsciousness of the three heads which precipitately bobbed down out of sight at their approach, while the owners of the heads coiled themselves up in the narrowest of corners, with much scraping of shoes on the boards, in the process.

"This old station is just full of rats," she continued, in a tone of careless explanation, as they passed the hiding-place of her brother and his friends. "I heard the ticket-man say, just before your train came in, that he was coming out with his gun to shoot some of them, as soon as the engine had backed down out of the way."

A long-drawn squeak, as of an animal in pain, answered to her words, and they went on, while Allie threw one triumphant glance over her shoulder at the three heads which had promptly reappeared as soon as her back was turned.

Once seated opposite her cousin in the carriage, while they waited for Mr. Burnam to join them, Allie could study his face at her ease, as she chattered away to him, in the hope of making him feel at home. He had attracted her at the first glance; and the more she looked at him the stronger became her impression that here was a cousin worth having. He was large of his age, finely formed, and taller than Howard, and had a frank, boyish face, which just now looked a little tired after his long journey, and a little troubled and nervous at coming among new friends. For the rest, he had a mass of soft, reddish-brown hair, a freckled face, firm red lips which parted, now and then, to show two rows of small, even teeth, and two deep dimples that came and went in his cheeks, and a pair of near-sighted brown eyes that looked very steadily into Allie's, as if trying to read his new kinswoman, and find out from her into what hands he was likely to fall.

And, indeed, he would have looked far that day without finding a more attractive cousin, for Allie, in her desire to play the hostess well, had dropped her usual rollicking manner, and assumed a sweet, childish dignity which became her as well as her more wonted gayety. Charlie's face cleared a little, as he looked into her great blue eyes and watched the changing expressions of her fresh young face, so pretty and bright in its soft, warm setting of fur.

"Why didn't Howard come down with you, daught?" asked Mr. Burnam, as he took his place beside them, and the carriage, turning from the station, drove away up the street towards the house.

For an instant, Allie's gaze was fixed on a distant opening between the buildings, where three boyish figures were scurrying along as fast as their feet could carry them. Then she roused herself, and turned to the lad before her, as if she had not heard her father's question.

"Didn't you have a good time on the way out here, Cousin Charlie?" she inquired hastily. "Howard and I have been envying you your journey."

"Can't say I enjoyed it," Charlie answered. "I'd never even travelled all night before, and it was no end lonesome, riding along, day in and day out, without a soul to speak to. An old friend of mother's met me in Chicago, and put me on the train for Council Bluffs, and 'twas easy enough changing there, so I didn't have any trouble; but you'd better believe I was glad to see Uncle Ralph when he walked into the sleeper yesterday afternoon."

"I believe I'd be willing to go round the world alone, if I could only go," said Allie. "I'm a real railroad man's daughter, and like to travel; don't I, poppy?" And she nestled closer to her father's side, while with amused eyes she watched their guest's expression change, first to astonishment, then to disgust, as he looked at the main street, with its low buildings, some few of brick, little one-story structures, whose fronts were run up in a thin, flat wall, with sham window blinds at a second-story level, to present the appearance of more pretentious buildings.

Fresh as he was from the closely-packed streets of the great city, with their unbroken rows of towering business blocks and apartment houses, Charlie was conscious of vague wonder at the rough little mining camp before him. Then he turned and looked up at the mountain, and, boy that he was, he forgot all else, all the crudeness of the buildings and all the roughness of the surroundings, as he saw the full grandeur of the snow-clad Rockies shining and glistening in the morning sunshine, which lay caressingly over their giants slopes. He bent forward to look at them once more, while his face grew very thoughtful and intent; then he dropped back into his old corner, saying, in an awed, hushed tone, as if to himself,--

"Jove! It's worth it all, to have a chance to look at those."

"I'm glad you like them," said Allie heartily, though she smiled at his "Jove," when she recalled her recent charge to Howard to avoid all slang. "The town must seem queer to you; but the mountains make up for it. Now lean 'way forward, and look out this side. That little brick house is ours; and there's mamma in the door, and Howard just back of her, waiting to give you greeting."

"Now, honestly, Allie, how did you like him?" Howard asked, as soon as his mother had taken Charlie to his room and the door closed behind them.

"I think I do like him," said Allie slowly. "He didn't talk much coming up; but I don't know as I wonder, when we're all strangers to him. He has sort of a good face; of course he isn't handsome, like Ned and Grant, but he looks as if he'd have some fun in him."

"I shouldn't think he did look like Ned," returned Howard disdainfully; "you don't often see anybody that does. This fellow has red hair, too, and I don't like that kind. He's dressed himself up regardless, in his derby hat and long-tailed ulster. Does he wear knickerbockers, Allie, or does he think he's too old for them?"

"How should I know?" answered Allie. "He's pretty long, and I began at the top, so I didn't get down so far; but when we are used to his freckles and his glasses, I don't think he'll seem so bad to us."

"You almost gave us away, with your rat speech," said Howard, laughing at the recollection. "Grant giggled till I was afraid Charlie'd hear him, so I squeaked to cover up the noise. You had us cornered there; and I didn't want to get caught, for I knew mammy wouldn't like it. She's been so anxious to have Charlie get here and have a good time with us, that I didn't want to spoil it all."

"How long have you been home?" asked his sister, as she turned away to go to her room and take off her jacket and hat.

"I had just time to drop off my coat, as I came in through the kitchen, and get to the front door, when you turned the corner. I believe mammy has spent the last hour between the door and window. I wonder what they're doing in there; I wish they'd hurry up, for I want some lunch. Charlie ought to be hungry, too, for he had breakfast at Argenta. Remember those elk steaks we had there last fall, sis?"

Allie made a wry face at the memory.

"Poor Charlie! He will think he's come into the wilderness. You should have seen his face, Howard, when we were driving up Main Street. It was too funny; he looked as if he didn't know whether to laugh or cry. He stood it very well till he came to the office; then that green sham front was too much for him, and he fairly groaned."

"I'll tell you what," Howard counselled her; "can't you get hold of him, and tell him about some of the ways we have out here, and get him used to it, so he won't show just what he thinks of us? Girls can do that sort of thing better than boys, and he'll need some coaching, of course. Just pussy-cat him a little; and then he looks as if he'd take any amount of advice. I don't care, for you and me;

but the Everetts won't stand anything of that kind. They've been here ever since the town started, and they think it's the only place in the world."

"'Tis one of the best," said Allie decisively. "Of course, 'tisn't pretty, nor very fine; but I've had the best times since I came here I ever had, and I'm not going to have anybody run it down when I'm round. I'll give him a talking-to this very night. Now, let's just come out and take one race to the corner and back; I've been proper as long as I can, and I must do something to let off steam. He's all out of the way and won't see me. Come on!" And away they went, racing down the street in the warm noon sun.

After his quiet talk with his aunt, who had gone with him to lead the way to his room, Charlie no longer felt any doubt of his welcome. Mrs. Burnam was so like his father in her manner, so bright and brisk, yet so gentle, that her nephew felt at ease with her at once. There had been something indescribably motherly in her face, as she sat down on the edge of the bed, and, taking his hand, drew him down at her side, while she questioned him about his journey, and the friends he had left behind him. Then she spoke of his mother so tenderly that the boy's lips quivered, and two great tears rolled down his cheeks. That was more than Mrs. Burnam's warm heart could bear. For a moment she let his fresh sorrow have its way; then she bent forward and put her arm around him, just as she might have done with Howard.

"I know, Charlie," she said gently, "nobody else can take her place; but, while you are with us, remember that you are our own boy, and are as much at home with us as Howard himself. And now come, if you're ready, and get acquainted with your cousins, while I see about the lunch."

As Charlie went back to the parlor once more, he was surprised to find the room deserted and the front door slightly open. With a little shiver of cold and loneliness, he stepped across the room to close the door, and stood still, to gaze in astonishment at the sight before him. Up the middle of the road came two figures, evidently engaged in some mad race. The boy he recognized at once as being his Cousin Howard; but who was the small Amazon who rushed along at his side, bareheaded and with her short, thick hair flying in the wind, as she easily kept pace with the longer strides of her brother? Surely, this could not be Allie, the demure little maid who had met him with such easy, quiet grace! Charlie knew little of girls and their ways; but he had always looked upon them with a certain distrust, as being all-absorbed in their fine clothes and their prim deportment. The few he had known in New York had done nothing to alter his opinion, and it had never before occurred to him as a possibility that a young girl could romp and run, and enjoy the free, out-of-door life which is the rightful privilege of every healthy child. This new revelation was quite to his liking, and his astonishment gave place to interest and then to delight, as Allie gradually outstripped her brother, and came flying up the steps far in advance of him, with a triumphant shout of laughter, just as her cousin appeared in the open doorway, loudly applauding her victory.

Early that evening Allie and her cousin were alone in the parlor, for Mrs. Burnam was putting Victor to bed, Mr. Burnam had gone down to his office for an hour, and Howard had gone out on an errand with the Everett boys. The afternoon had been devoted to helping Charlie to unpack and settle himself in his new quarters; and over this informal occupation their acquaintance had made rapid strides, so it was with a sense of duty well-performed that Allie curled herself up in the great easy-chair before the pine knots blazing on the andirons, and turned to look at the boy, pacing up and down the room. Divested of his long ulster, which had called forth Howard's criticism, her cousin stood before her, dressed, like many another boy, in the light brown suit of the period, but with a grace of position and pride of carriage which had made him a noticeable lad, even in the great city school, where he had only been one of scores of well-dressed, well-trained boys. Allie studied him for a moment in silence; then she gave a little contented nod to herself, as she said interrogatively,--

"Well, Charlie?"

"Well?" he responded, as he came to a halt at her chair, and, folding his arms on the back, stood looking down at her while she raised her face to his.

"What were you thinking about?" she demanded. "Were you homesick or tired, that made you look so sober?"

"I was thinking about New York," he answered candidly; "wondering about some of the fellows in our school. They were a jolly set, and I'd like to see them; but I'm not homesick a bit. I think I'm going to like it here, when I get used to it."

"I suppose it does seem very strange to you," mused Allie, as if to herself, while she watched the face above her, looking so thoughtful in the flickering light. Then she added abruptly, "Come round where I can talk to you, Charlie; I've something very important to say to you."

"Yes, ma'am," he answered, but without stirring from his place.

"Come," she insisted, patting the broad arm of her chair with an inviting gesture. "I want to give you your first lesson in Western life; and I can't talk to you half so well, when you're just back of me. If I can't watch you, I sha'n't know when you're getting vexed and wishing I'd stop."

"All right; fire ahead." And Charlie moved around to her side, where he clasped his hands and brought his spectacles to bear upon her with an owlish solemnity.

"That's a very good boy," said his cousin approvingly. Then she continued, in a tone of elderly counsel, "Now, my dear child, I am about to say a few words to you which shall be for your own good."

"Oh, I say," remonstrated Charlie, his dignity breaking down all at once; "how old are you, Allie,--sixty, or seventy-five?"

"You shouldn't laugh," returned Allie, shaking her head at him reproachfully. "That's just the way Mrs. Pennypoker talks to Ned and Grant; I've heard her, lots of times. But now, truly, I wish you'd be good and listen to me, for I do want to tell you something that will be a help to you. The people out here are different from those you've seen, and the ways aren't like those farther east. I don't know why 'tis, but they hate to be reminded of it, and, when we came here, papa told us never to say anything bad about the town, as if we didn't like it, for we'd get everybody down on us. We did like it, though, so we didn't have to fib. But now you're here you'd better just keep still about anything that strikes you funny, when you're off with the boys. Then you can come back and talk it over with me, when they aren't round, if you want to; I don't mind; only don't let Howard hear you, for he'd tell the Everetts. See? That's all; but I thought I'd warn you."

"You're a trump, Allie; and I'll try not to disgrace you," said Charlie gratefully. "Of course, it seems awfully queer to me; but I won't give it away, if I can help it. What's the matter now?" he demanded, as Allie leaned back in her chair and burst into a peal of laughter.

"I was just thinking how funny 'twas," she answered; "only this morning I was telling the boys that their slang would shock you, and they must drop it; but here you are, every bit as bad as they. I don't believe there's so much difference between Montana and New York, after all."

"'Tisn't the place, it's boys," responded Charlie sagely. "They're pretty much the same, wherever you take them. I think the difference is in the girls, and, if you please, I believe I prefer the Western ones."

Allie flushed rosy red at the unexpected compliment, but before she had time to enjoy it, or to reply, there came a sudden knock at the dining-room door, and Janey's black face peered in at the crack.

"Miss Allie, honey," she said in a wheedling tone, as she rolled up her great eyes at her little mistress, "cyarn you get time to write a letter for me, bymeby?"

"I'll come out as soon as Mr. Howard gets home, Janey," she answered; then, as the head vanished and the door closed, she added to her cousin, "Janey can't read nor write, so I have to do all her letters for her. She's engaged to marry a man in Washington, and she says he's 'in de guv'ment.' His name is Hamilton Lincoln Cornwallis; but he lives at number seven and a half Goat Alley, so I don't believe he's President yet. You've no idea how funny his letters are. Maybe she'll get you to read one, some day."

CHAPTER III.

THE EVERETT HOUSEHOLD.

Mrs. Euphemia Pennypoker belonged to that unpleasant type of individuals whose members, for lack of specific excellence, are commonly spoken of by their friends as "thoroughly estimable women." She possessed all the virtues, but none of the graces which make virtue attractive to the youthful mind; and she regulated her daily life by a cast-iron code that was as unvarying and heartless as the smile which sixty years of habit had stamped upon her thin, bloodless lips. Mrs. Pennypoker was said to have been handsome in her day, handsome with an austere, cold beauty; but her day was long past, and the only remaining trace of her good looks lay in her piercing gray eyes, and her long, straight Greek nose. The eyes were undimmed by time; but the crow's-feet had gathered thick about them, and the Greek nose was surmounted by a pair of large, round eye-glasses, which only served to intensify the sternness of the eyes behind them. To the children around her, there was something awe-inspiring in those eye-glasses, and in the broad black ribbon which held them suspended about her neck. In times of peace, they had the appearance of being on the watch for some hidden sin; but when occasion for punishment arose, there was something positively terrifying in their glare, and the culprit longed for his last hour to come, that he might escape from their power.

Dame Nature had been in a generous mood when she had endowed Mrs. Pennypoker, for she had given her a massive frame and constitution of bronze, which made her thoroughly intolerant of those unfortunates who were not similarly blessed. But, impressive as Mrs. Pennypoker was in most respects, there was yet one undignified peculiarity which marred the otherwise perfect majesty of her appearance. Like Samson, her vulnerable point lay in her hair; or, more properly speaking, in her lack of it. The ravages of time had removed a part of her dark brown locks, and left an oval bald spot, closely resembling the tonsure of a Romish priest. This defect was usually covered with an elaborate pile of braids and puffs; but occasionally the slippery surface of her bald crown and the power of gravitation proved too much for her hair-pins, and the whole structure slipped backward, to reveal a shining expanse of milk-white skin, gleaming forth from the dark tresses surrounding it. Moreover, rumor had been known to whisper that there was something peculiar about the rich brown hue of Mrs. Pennypoker's hair; that it was remarkable for a person of her age to be so free from the silver threads common among far younger women; and that, strangest of all, she was subject to periodical variations of color, her hair turning gray at the ends and then resuming its original tint, while, incredible as it might seem, the change always appeared at the ends nearest her scalp, though the tips of her hairs retained all their wonted lustre.

Coming from far-away New England, Mrs. Pennypoker was true to the blood of her Puritan ancestry. She had in her composition much of the stuff of which martyrs are made. She could have gone to the stake for her opinions; but she could just as cheerfully have turned the tables, and piled the fagots high about the misguided heretics who ventured to disagree with her own peculiar doctrines. Ever on the alert to find out the path of duty and to walk in it, she had promptly accepted the proposition of her distant cousin, Mr. Everett, to become his housekeeper, after the death of his wife; and, forsaking all her old associations, she had girded herself and her trunks, and, with her parrot as her sole companion, she had retired to the wilderness to subdue the dragons of anarchy and chaos which had probably entered into the Everett household.

Her first dragon proved to be a very long-tailed one; and though he was promptly met, he was by no means so promptly subdued. An hour after her arrival, she had penetrated to the kitchen, where she was suddenly confronted by Wang Kum, the shoe-button-eyed Chinaman who had been in the service of Mrs. Everett for months before her death. In their first interview, Mrs. Pennypoker was ignominiously routed and driven from the field, for Wang Kum ignored her stony gaze, and cheerfully and volubly chattered to her in a torrent of Pidgin-English which left her no opportunity for reply; so she withdrew, resolving that her first reform should be the removal of Wang from office. However, on this question Mr. Everett was determined; Wang Kum had been their faithful servant, and knew the ways of their household; moreover, he had been devoted to Mrs. Everett during her last illness, and in that kitchen Wang Kum should stay. Defeated in this main object, Mrs. Pennypoker next devoted herself to the task of civilization, and waged daily warfare with the Chinaman, in her endeavors to convert him to American ways and dress, and Calvinistic theology.

"Old lady heap talkee; Wang Kum no care," he used to confide to Louise Everett, after an unusually long and tedious fray. "Wang min' Miss Lou; old lady too flesh."

Four years before this time, when the Blue Creek copper mine was opened and the building of the great smelter had brought to the creek the first settlers of the mining camp, Mr. Everett had been made superintendent of the mine, and had brought his family out to be with him. Of his three children, Louise was now in the first flush of young womanhood, a pretty, graceful blonde of twenty, who had been educated in an Eastern school until the sudden death of her mother had called her home to take charge of the housekeeping, before Mrs. Pennypoker appeared upon the scene, to relieve her of the care, and act as matron to watch over her young cousin with an eagle eye. For the past few years, Louise had been away from home so much of the time that the loss of her mother fell less heavily upon her than on her young brothers, who had been the constant companions of the bright, pretty little woman who had devoted her life to theirs.

Mrs. Pennypoker was scarcely the person to make good their loss; and Ned and Grant would have had a lonely life, had it not been for motherly Mrs. Burnam, whose heart was large enough to take in all the children with whom she came in contact. The Everetts were likable boys, too, just the companions she would have chosen for Howard and Allie: gay and mischievous, as every healthy boy should be, but with the high sense of honor and firm principle which can only come from a good mother and careful home training. Ned, the older one, at thirteen was the image of his father, with a rich, dark beauty which made him a striking contrast to Grant's light yellow hair and pink and white cheeks. Grant was his mother's own boy, in all but his eyes, which were like his father's, large and brown; and he had received his mother's maiden name, just as he had received the features and complexion of her family.

Of all the members of the Everett household, Grant was the only one who felt no fear of Mrs. Pennypoker. Even his father was far more in subjection to her rule than was his little son. Grant had been the first to discover her bald spot-- which he promptly christened her storm centre--and to call Ned's attention to it; and therein lay much of his power over her. Now, whenever Mrs. Euphemia threatened to get the better of him, he had only to fix his eyes steadily on the top of her head, or abstractedly rub his hand over his own yellow pate, to cause her to abandon her lecture and escape to her mirror, in order to assure herself that all was as it should be.

The Everetts lived a little to the west of the Burnam's, in what was usually spoken of as "one of the old houses," to distinguish it from the more modern structures of brick and boards. This particular old house was, in fact, the oldest one in the camp, for it had been built by the superintendent for his family, when the other inhabitants of the place were still living in tents pitched along the edge of the creek. Like most of the other houses of the town, it was a one-story building, low and rambling, with odd wings and projections, which had been added to the original square structure as the needs of the family demanded. It was built of rough-hewn logs, but the front was coated with clapboards, in deference to the prevailing style of architecture, which literally put its best foot forward.

Within, the walls were guiltless of lath or plaster, but were covered with strips of cotton cloth, to which the wall-paper was pasted. At certain seasons, this imparted a peculiar effect to the rooms, for, in the fierce winter gales, occasional breezes would work their way through the crannies of the wall and cause the paper and its cloth background to sway backwards and forwards, to the horror of the stranger unused to such modes of finish, since the sight of the walls swaying and wriggling before his eyes could only be satisfactorily explained as the result of intoxication, or of temporary insanity. The same stranger would have stopped short in surprise, on entering the Everetts' clumsy log-house. In spite of its unattractive exterior, it was a cosy, luxurious dwelling, with furniture, draperies and pictures which would do credit to any Eastern city house; for Mrs. Everett had loved pretty things, and had gathered them about her in the hope of making home the spot most enjoyable for her children.

The Everetts were gathered around the table for their late dinner, one night in February, soon after Charlie's arrival in Blue Creek. At the head of the table sat Mrs. Pennypoker, who never appeared so majestic as when she was presiding over the bountifully spread board, for Mrs. Pennypoker was what is known as a liberal provider, and had a lingering fondness, herself, for the good things of this earth. To-night, she was unusually benign, for Wang Kum had outdone himself, and the soup was the perfection of flavoring, the roast done to a turn; so she could relax her anxious scrutiny of the appointments of the table, and lend an ear to what Mr. Everett was saying to his daughter.

"Yes, Mr. Nelson came down to the office to see me to-day. It seems he's been talking up the matter of a boy choir, and he wants Ned and Grant, here, to sing in it. He's going to have Howard, and he's heard that Charlie sings; then there are about a dozen little German fellows, and some men. I told him I'd no objection, and I'd ask the boys what they thought."

"He said something about it to me, after service last night," answered Louise, who acted as organist at the little Episcopal chapel. "He said he wanted to get his plans all made as soon as he could, so we could go to work on the vestments and begin training, to have the choir ready to sing at Easter. I told him that both the boys sang, but I didn't know what you'd say to it."

"I'm willing," Mr. Everett was beginning, when Mrs. Pennypoker interrupted him.

"Do you mean," she asked with icy distinctness, as she leaned forward over the table to add emphasis to her words, "that you are going to let your sons sing in one of those choirs that march into church with their night-gowns on, and singsong the answers to what the priest says?"

"Why, yes," said Mr. Everett, smiling at his cousin, in the hope of calming her disgust. "Yes; that is, if that's what you call it. The boys both have good voices, and it certainly won't hurt them any, for Mr. Nelson knows how to train them well."

"Humph!" returned Mrs. Pennypoker uncompromisingly. "It's my belief that they'd much better go to hear good old Dr. Hornblower, and let this flummery alone. Your Nelson man is no better than a papist, with his colored windows and his chants and all; and, now he's succeeded in getting his new chapel, there'll be no stopping him."

"Just watch the storm centre," whispered Grant to his brother, as Mrs. Pennypoker ended her remark with an expressive, but ill-advised shake of her head. "It's coming into action fast."

"I am glad you feel satisfied with the doctor," answered Mr. Everett, looking squarely into the face of his irate relative. "He is doubtless a good man; but my wife was a member of Mr. Nelson's church, and her children have always been accustomed to going there, so I think they would better continue. Another thing I started to tell you, Lou," he went on, as he turned to his daughter again, "I hear that, at last, Blue Creek is to have a new doctor. There's a young fellow from one of the Eastern colleges on his way out here to settle. The Fullertons know him, and say he's a brilliant man. It's about time we had somebody, for since old Dr. Meacham died, nobody's dared be ill, for fear they'd die before a doctor could get over from Butte."

"And when this one comes, we're all going to celebrate by being ill; is that what you mean, papa?" Louise asked playfully, as she shook her head at Grant, who was stretching up, to peer curiously at the top of Mrs. Pennypoker's head, where a pale crescent was gradually appearing and waxing wider. "When's he coming?"

"Not for five or six weeks," her father answered; "so you'll have to keep well for a while longer. He's on his way; but he's going to visit some friends in Omaha and Denver, before he gets here."

"Hullo!" exclaimed Ned suddenly.

"What's struck you?" asked Grant.

"Nothing; only I was wondering if this could be the same man Charlie Mac was telling about. He met a young man on the train, papa, who came from Chicago to the Bluffs with him. He had next section, so they talked some, and he told Charlie he was from way back East, and was coming to Blue Creek, too. He said he'd never been here, and asked Charlie all manner of questions about the place and all."

"I don't believe he found out much," said Grant with a giggle. "Charlie hadn't any more idea than a dead man what 'twas going to be like out here."

"No; but he's done pretty well since he came, though," said Ned admiringly. "He's acted as if 'twere just what he'd always been used to. It's my belief that Allie's been coaching him; he'd never get on so well by himself, I know."

"He came pretty near finishing himself, the second day he was here, all the same," added Grant. "Did you hear about it, papa? Nobody'd told him to look out a little, till he was used to this air. He started out to run, and it used him up in no time, so he turned blue-white, and nearly dropped. He's taking it slowly, now; and is getting into it by little and little."

"By the way," asked Louise suddenly; "what has become of Marjorie? I haven't seen her for a week."

"She's under punishment," replied Ned lugubriously; "and we haven't any of us seen her since the afternoon we were out skating, just before Charlie came. I don't know exactly what 'tis; but it must be something pretty bad, for her mother to keep her away so long."

"Marjorie is always getting herself into trouble, it seems to me," said Mr. Everett, laughing indulgently as he spoke, for he had a genuine liking for this active, flyaway young girl, whose heart was as true and kind as her impulses were hasty and rash.

"So she is," returned Ned defensively; "but she flies into everything head first, and without thinking much about it; and then she goes into the depths of gunny-sacks and cinders afterwards, when it's too late to do any good."

"That isn't a very helpful kind of penitence," remarked Mrs. Pennypoker, looking up from her plate.

"It's a very natural one, I am afraid," said Mr. Everett charitably. "Then Marjorie hasn't seen this new friend of yours?"

"No, not yet," Grant answered. "It's a shame, too, for she was in a hurry to get a look at him. He is a first-rate fellow, really, papa; and doesn't seem a bad tenderfoot, even to old-timers like Ned and me. What do you want, Wang?" he added, as Wang Kum's head appeared at the door.

"Mas' How'd, he here," announced Wang briefly. "He no come in; wan' you." And he vanished, followed by the boys, who hurried out in search of their friend.

In the mean time, at the Burnam's a short conversation was taking place, which would have enlightened the boys on the subject of Charlie's easy adaptability to his new surroundings. It was his habit to practise for an hour after dinner each night, and Allie was usually beside him. She loved music as well as did her cousin, and was content to settle herself on a wide sofa drawn up beside the piano, sometimes with a book, but more often idly leaning back against the cushions, with her eyes fixed on her cousin's face, as he gradually lost all consciousness of her presence in his enjoyment of the music. Young boy as he was, and a normal, healthy boy, too, Charlie had undoubted genius in this one direction, and added to a rare talent for music the skill gained by five years of study under the best master that the city could afford, until, both in subject and method, his playing was far beyond what one would naturally expect in a lad of his years. It had been a great delight to him to find that Allie cared for his music, and could understand the varying moods which he tried to express in his hours of practice. The two cousins really had their best times in these nightly visits, for when his regular time of practice was over, Charlie would still linger at the piano, playing in a soft, fitful undertone, while they discussed the events of the day, or planned for the morrow's program. The week they had been together had quickly ripened their first liking for each other into a close friendship; and after a day of out-of-door frolics with the other boys, Charlie had learned to look forward to the time of talking it over with Allie, and listening to her merry, whimsical comments on what they had done and seen. But, on this particular night, Charlie was bound on gaining information.

"If you please, ma'am," he began, as he let his hands fall from the keys, and turned to face his cousin.

"Oh--yes--what?" responded Allie, gradually rousing herself from her story.

"If you please, I'd like to ask a question," he said meekly. "I'm in want of a few pointers."

"Well?" and Allie was all attention, as she smiled up at her cousin's perplexed face.

"In the first place, how much is a bit?" demanded Charlie.

"Twelve and a half cents," she answered promptly. "Why?"

"I don't know as I dare tell," Charlie replied, with a shamefaced laugh.

"Go on," urged Allie curiously. "I'm sure it's something funny, and you know I never tell tales."

"Well, if you'll promise, true blue. You see, I wanted some new rubbers, for mine were all full of holes, and I was tired of going round with wet feet; so I went down town this morning and tried to buy some. The clerk said they were six bits, but I didn't know how much that was, and didn't want to say so, so I told him that I didn't quite like the kind, and went off."

"You've a great mind, Charlie," said Allie approvingly. "Everybody here counts by bits; two make a quarter; and then, you know, we don't have any pennies here, nothing smaller than a five-cent piece. Remember that, and don't offer anybody a penny, even if it's a beggar. Go on; what next?"

"That's about all, for this time," he answered. "Oh, no; there's one thing more. What's that queer place down south of here, all fenced in, and with little bits of log cabins scattered around as if they'd just been dropped out of a pepper-box?"

"That's Chinatown," said Allie, laughing at the accuracy of the description. "We must get papa to take us there, some day. But now I want to tell you something. You know Marjorie Fisher?"

"Can't say I do," returned Charlie flippantly.

"Yes, I know what you mean," interrupted Allie; "but you know who she is, and you want to know her, herself, for she's great fun. She's been--busy, this last week; but I had a note from her to-night, and she wants us all to come down there to-morrow afternoon for a candy-pull. I told her we'd go, so she's going to stop here after school and wait for you and Howard, and we'll all go on together. The Everetts will be there, too, and we shall be sure to have a good time; we always do at Marjorie's."

CHAPTER IV.

ON THE CROSS-HEAD.

"The bees and the wasps were there. The old queen bee, with fiendish glee, Was pulling a hornet's hair. The monkey thought 'twas rough; He took a pinch of snuff, And then the bees began to sneeze, And left,"--

sang a clear, boyish voice outside, and the next moment steps were heard on the piazza.

"Who's that?" asked Marjorie, glancing up from the skating cap, which, with infinite pains, she was crocheting, in thoughtful anticipation of Howard's birthday, the following summer.

"Charlie; don't you know his voice?" responded Allie, who was sitting with one foot tucked under her, while she sewed the buttons on her shoe.

"How should I? I've never heard him sing," answered Marjorie.

"You will soon, for he and Ned are to lead the new choir at Easter. Charlie seems to be feeling unusually comf'y to-day," said his cousin, as the boy came in at the side door opening into the dining-room, and walked over to the corner where they were sitting, curled up by the stove. "Where'd you get that pretty song?" she added.

"Made it up, of course; didn't you know I was a poet?" inquired Charlie blandly, while he nodded to Marjorie, and then pulled off his glasses to wipe away the steam condensed on them by the sudden change from the cold outer air to the heat within the house.

"I never should have supposed so," Marjorie answered, laughing. "You look altogether too plump and well-fed."

"Can't help it; you can't tell by looking at a toad how far he'll hop. I wrote it 'all my lone,' as Vic says," responded Charlie. "I'm very proud of it, too."

"Sit down and amuse us," said Allie, hospitably drawing a chair nearer the fire.

"No, thank you; I'm engaged, and must be going," returned Charlie, with a lofty air of importance which was not without its effect upon his cousin.

"What's going on?" she asked curiously. "I told Marjorie that you acted unusually set up over something."

"I met Mr. Everett just now, and he told me that, if I'd get over to the smelter at three, he'd let me go down the mine this afternoon."

"O Charlie, take us with you," begged his cousin, starting up, forgetful of the fact that she was still without one shoe. "I've never been, and I do want to go, so much."

"Can't; girls aren't invited," said Charlie heartlessly. "He did say that he'll take us all at once, though, as soon as they put the cage in, next month; but he doesn't like to take but one at a time, on this thing they're running now. I wish you could go, for 'twould be lots more fun."

"'Tisn't much to go down," said Marjorie, with an air of superior wisdom. "It's dark and slippery, and not any too clean; and you have to get out of the way of something or other, most every minute."

"Yes, I know," said Allie; "it's all very well to say that, when you've been; but I never had a chance to go. I was ill the time Howard went; and now I shall be the only one left that hasn't been down. I hope you'll have an awfully good time, though, Charlie, and not get lost, or smashed, or anything else that's bad, while you're underground. Isn't it growing colder?" she added, as Charlie turned up the collar of his ulster and scientifically pinched the edges of his ears, preparatory to starting out once more.

"'T isn't exactly balmy," he answered. "Want anything, before I go?" And a moment later the door closed behind him.

"You're a lucky girl, Allie," said Marjorie, while she watched the figure striding along down the road. "Even Ned says he's the jolliest fellow in town, all but Howard."

"Yes, 't is good to have him here," said Allie contentedly, as she slipped on her shoe and stooped to button it up. "He's just as good-natured and nice as he can be; and I think I like him better than any boy I ever saw, except Howard, even if he hasn't been here quite a month."

"Not better than Ned?" Marjorie exclaimed incredulously.

"Well--no--I don't know," said Allie, wavering a little. "Ned's just about as near right as he can be; but I believe, after all, I'd rather live in the house with Charlie. Ned might be a little too peppery for a steady diet."

"I never thought you'd turn a cold shoulder to Ned," said Marjorie, shaking her head over Allie's defection. "Charlie's very nice and gentlemanly, and all that, but I don't believe he has half Ned's pluck. Do you remember the time he sprained his wrist falling off his pony, way up the gulch, and wouldn't tell of it till we were home again? I don't think Charlie Mac would stand that kind of thing long. There's no special reason he shouldn't be agreeable; we've all of us tried our best to make him have a good time."

"Charlie isn't a baby, though," returned Allie, valiantly rising to the defence of her cousin. "You think, just because he knows more about music than 'most anybody else in the camp, and looks and acts as if he came from a city, that he's more than half girl. But I'll tell you he isn't, Marjorie, and if anything came to try him, you'd find he'd come up to the mark every bit as well as Ned. I don't know as I care to have anything happen, though, just for the sake of proving it."

In the mean time, the subject of the conversation was walking rapidly in the direction of the smelter, whose pile of huge red buildings lay a little to the southeast of the town, across the creek and close to the foot of the mountain which towered above it sheer and straight. A few hundred feet down the cañon below it, and a little farther back from the creek, was the shaft leading down into the mine, and beside it the engine house with the machinery needful for raising the ore, and for carrying the miners to and from the cross-cuts, hundreds of feet below.

Though he had often been to the smelter with Ned and Grant, it was the first time that Charlie had visited the place alone. He felt very small and insignificant, as he stepped inside the enclosure, with its array of great buildings, mammoth chimneys whence rose the smoke from countless and undying fires, and its throng of busy workers. Then he entered the little building which served as superintendent's office, and in a moment the whir and clang of the outer life was left behind him, and he found himself in a quiet, pleasant room, with only a collection of maps and photographs and specimens of ores, to tell of the vast business centering there. As the boy shyly came in at the door, Mr. Everett rose to receive him.

"O Charlie, you're just on the minute, and I'm all ready for you," he said, glancing up at the clock.

"Somers, I'm going down the shaft with this young man; if anybody wants me, tell him I'll be here at five." And, putting on his overcoat, he went away, followed by Charlie, who was filled with an eager enthusiasm at the idea of going so far towards the center of the earth.

"I'm sorry," Mr. Everett said, as they followed a path winding in and out among the buildings, and then came out on the main road leading to the shaft; "I'm sorry that we haven't time to take in the smelter, too, to-day; but you can go there almost any time. Any of the men in the office can take you through it, as well as I can; but I don't let strangers go into the mine unless I'm with them. We're going to put in a new cage, next month," he added casually, as they drew near the shaft.

"What's that for?" asked Charlie, to whom cages and their construction were a mystery.

"Safer, and can carry more," answered his host concisely. "These cross-heads and buckets are slow work. A two-deck cage will do the same amount in much less time, and there's no fear of their catching, as these do sometimes."

As he spoke, they paused to look at the gearing of windlass and cable at the mouth of the shaft; then Charlie cautiously approached the opening. After all he had heard of mines and shafts, it was rather disappointing to him to see only a great, square hole leading down into the depths of the earth. What he had expected, it would be hard to say; but it is certain that his disappointment deepened when, after three strokes from the engineer's bell, the hoisting engine suddenly started into life, and, out from the darkness of the shaft, there slowly emerged into view an ungainly contrivance of four great timbers, arranged in a hollow square and hung on a cable, which passed freely through openings in the upper and lower timbers, to carry a huge bucket fastened to its end, while a black-faced miner stood in the bucket, much in the attitude of a jack-in-the-box after the spring is loosed.

"That's what we call the cross-head, above," explained Mr. Everett. "It slides free on the rope, and rests on the fastening of the bucket. Now you see how we bring up the ore."

"But do we have to go down in that thing?" inquired Charlie, drawing back in disgust, as he surveyed the grimy, dusty bucket before him.

"Not unless you prefer it," Mr. Everett answered, laughing. "It's against rules to ride in it; and anyway I usually go on the cross-head, myself, for the bucket reminds me too much of Simple Simon. Step on here," he added, as the crude elevator sank down until the upper beam was on a level with the surface of the ground. "Now, if you just hold on to the rope, you're all right. Let us go slowly,

Joe," he went on, to the waiting engineer; "I want to take a look at the shaft, as we go down. We'll try the seven-hundred level to-day."

A moment later, they began to sink away from the light above them, while the opening at the mouth of the shaft grew smaller and smaller to their eyes, and their lamps only cast a sickly, uncertain light on the walls beside them. They went down slowly, so slowly, that, as soon as he had had time to accustom himself to the new sensation, Charlie had plenty of opportunity to examine the walls. For the most part, they were roughly cased with boards and surrounded at intervals by the massive collar-timbers, projecting ten or twelve inches inside the boards. At each side of the shaft were the heavy upright guides, running from top to bottom and serving to keep in place the cross-head, which was fitted to move easily between them. Down, down they went, for what seemed to the boy a limitless distance. They had passed a great square chamber, opening into along, lighted corridor which Mr. Everett had told him were the station and cross-cut at the four-hundred level, and still they were sinking. All at once they came to a sudden stop, and the next instant Charlie felt the rope he was holding slowly drawing down through his hands. Mr. Everett gave a quick exclamation.

"Let go the rope!" he commanded abruptly.

"I'm perfectly willing," answered Charlie, laughing, as he rubbed his tingling palms. "What's up, anyway? We don't seem to be anywhere in particular."

"We're caught a little," replied Mr. Everett quietly. "You needn't be frightened, for it's happened before. All is, the cross-head has caught, and the bucket is going down without us, and taking the rope with it. Have you a steady head?"

"I s'pose so," said Charlie lightly, for, in his ignorance of mines, he had no idea of the possible danger of his position.

"Very well; can you turn around and step down on the beam that's just below us?" returned Mr. Everett, still speaking in the same calm voice, though with the brevity of a captain giving his orders on a field of battle. "If you can, do it, and then put your arm around the back of the guide there. So; that's all right."

In another moment, he had followed Charlie, and taken his place beside him on the other side of the guide, where he showed the boy how to grasp the timber in such a way that the cross-head, coming up, should not touch his arm. That done, he breathed a sigh of relief.

"There!" he said; "now we're safe for the time being. The next question is: how are we going to get out of this trap?"

"Why couldn't we stay on the cross-head?" asked Charlie, as it began to move slowly away from the spot where it had lodged.

"Just that reason," returned Mr. Everett, with a motion of his head towards the clumsy frame which, once loosed, went sliding away down the rope after the bucket. "Though you may not have known it, young man, you were never in a much more dangerous place than you were five minutes ago; for, as soon as it could get free, the cross-head was going to crash down on top of the bucket, with force enough to kill anybody that happened to be on it. I knew 'twould go, sooner or later; but I didn't feel so sure that we could get off in time."

"Then it's done it before?" asked Charlie, in no wise moved by the knowledge of his past danger, but, boy-like, rather enjoying the novelty of his position, halfway down the shaft of the mine, and lodged like a fly on the wall, with only a narrow beam between himself and a fall of four or five hundred feet.

"Once," answered Mr. Everett, amused, in spite of his anxiety, by the boy's coolness. "It killed four men on the cross-head, and the one in the bucket; but they have such accidents in the other mines often enough, so we know about what the chances are. That's one reason we're going to put in a cage. Now," he went on, resuming his tone of authority, "don't you try to move, and, above all, don't look down. I'm going to get round to the other side, where I can reach the bell-rope, and signal the engineer to bring up the cross-head again."

"Not walk around on this beam!" exclaimed Charlie, as his interest changed to genuine alarm, for he realized that such an attempt was a very different matter from standing quiet and holding on by the upright timber between them.

"There's no other way," Mr. Everett answered, as he started on his perilous journey. "I can't reach to signal, from this side, and they never would find us without. We can't very well stay here, so that seems to be the only thing I can do. You needn't be alarmed, my boy," he added kindly, as he saw that the lad was now thoroughly frightened for his safety. "I am used to all these ins and outs, and know about what I can do, even if I never happened to get caught just here before. We miners get to be half monkeys, and can hang on where most men would fall."

He cautiously moved away a few inches along the beam; then he turned back to add one parting caution.

[Illustration: "He cautiously moved away a few inches along the beam."]

"Remember," he said, "and don't try to look down, even if you think you hear the cross-head coming up again. If you do, you are likely to get dizzy and fall."

How long it took for Mr. Everett to creep around the shaft, neither he nor Charlie ever knew. To them both, the moments seemed long, but to Mr. Everett, in particular, they were like hours, for he realized so keenly all the danger of their position, and felt the added responsibility for the young boy in his care. Inch by inch, step by step, he worked his way forward, until at length he reached the opposite guide, and felt the signal cord between his fingers. Then he knew that all trouble was ended.

One, two, three! rang out the engineer's bell.

The engineer was perplexed. He had been lowering the bucket more and more slowly, and still there had reached him no summons to stop, although his dial told him that the cross-head must be far below the seven-hundred level. And now came the summons to raise slowly, when he was sure that it was near the level of no station. What was the matter? It was evident that there was some trouble.

Slowly the engine drew up the bucket. It had passed the six-hundred level, then the five, and was now half way to the four-hundred, when the bell rang again, a single stroke this time, the order to stop. The engine was left motionless for some moments, while the engineer, with an anxious face, stood awaiting a fresh signal. He knew that something was wrong, and that it must concern the superintendent, since he had been the last man to go down. He spoke a few quick words to his assistant, and in a moment more a little crowd had gathered at the mouth of the shaft, just as the bell sounded again, three strokes.

Standing once more on the cross-head, Mr. Everett and Charlie could feel the man's excitement in the very motion of their tiny platform, as, obedient to the engine, it rose a little, then stopped, then rose again, as if feeling its way over an uncertain course. So they went on till the four-hundred level was below them; then the engine quickened its action. Little by little the tiny dot above them broadened, and turned to a wide disk of blue sky; and their lamps dwindled to a pale yellow before the clear light of day, as the cross-head, with its living freight, slowly came up into the bright air, amid the shouts of the men who stood waiting to receive it.

"Father said Joe was badly rattled," Ned told Charlie, that night, on their way to a choir rehearsal. "He was sure 'twas all up with you, and came near losing his head, so he couldn't run the engine, or answer a signal."

"I didn't suppose 'twas as bad as that," returned Charlie. "I didn't much like your father's having to walk round on that beam, or whatever you call it, but I thought the rest was good fun."

"I told father that I didn't believe you knew enough to be scared," said Ned, with masculine frankness. "He was talking, all dinner-time, about the way you kept cool and didn't make a fuss. Father was frightened, himself; he's never been in such a fix before, with all he's had to do with mines, and he says he's going to hurry now, to get that cage put in before they get into any more scrapes. But I just wish I'd been down there with you," he added enviously. "It's ever so much more fun than 'tis to go straight down, without any hitches."

"I'll wait till I've tried both, before I make up my mind," responded Charlie, as they reached the door of the chapel, and turned to wait for Howard and Grant to overtake them.

CHAPTER V.

THE MEETING IN THE WATERS.

Three weeks had passed since Charlie's unsuccessful attempt to explore the inside of a mine, and now the last of March had come. Already the boy had begun to feel as much at home with his cousins and in the mining camp, as if he had always lived in Blue Creek. Had the change from his old surroundings been less abrupt and marked, he might have had occasional twinges of homesickness; but everything about him was so new and strange, and so full of interest, that it left him no opportunity to mourn for his former life, save when the memory of his mother and of his loss of her came fresh upon him, to bring him an hour of keen sorrow. And now, as the weeks went on, although he never forgot her, still he learned to turn to his aunt for a sympathy and guidance which in a measure replaced the love that his mother had lavished upon him; while, on her side, Mrs. Burnam soon came to look on him quite as her own boy, and daily rejoiced in the close intimacy which had sprung up between Charlie and his cousins.

The time had been as busy as it was happy. In the absence of any good schools in the camp, Howard and the Everett boys studied under the supervision of Mr. Nelson, who gave up his mornings to them; and Charlie had joined them the week after he reached Blue Creek. Marjorie and Allie, too, went every morning to have a few simple lessons from the widow of one of Mr. Everett's former clerks,--a gentle, low-voiced Southern woman who, left alone to make her own way in this new country, was glad to help support herself by taking occasional private pupils. Accordingly, at a little before nine o'clock every morning, the procession of six formed in front of the Everetts and marched down the street for half a mile, where they separated, to go to their different tutors for three or four hours of work.

The unvarying program of the morning was followed by a hasty lunch; and, after that, there were few afternoons when the children did not meet. There were rare hours on the ice, when the skating was good; there was coasting such as Charlie had never dreamed of before, for in a country where all the land stood up on edge, as Grant expressed it, and where fences were unknown, it was easy to find the long, smooth slopes which are the delight of every owner of a good sled. Best of all, to Charlie's mind, were the long afternoons of running on snow-shoes, when they explored the cañon far to the north and south, or penetrated the deep, narrow gulch at the west of the camp. This last sport was especially delightful to the boy, for it gave him a wild sense of exhilaration to go sliding and scuffling along over three or four feet of snow, or coast lazily down the tiny hillocks in his path; and, under the instructions of his cousins, he quickly became skilled in the use of his runners, until he could easily hold his place at the head of the party, or turn a sharp corner without treading on his own or his neighbor's heels.

All this was excellent fun while it lasted, but far too soon came the time of melting snows, when skates and sleds and snow-shoes all had to be laid aside to wait for another winter. It had been a season of exceptionally deep snow, and the firm, hard crust lasted far past its usual time for thawing. Then came the chinook, the warm south wind, which eats away the accumulated snow of months in as many days; and the great white banks first grew porous, and then slowly sank away, while the water ran in streams along the streets, or lingered in still pools far under the unbroken crust, waiting to drench the unwary passerby who should venture to set foot upon their treacherous covering.

It was the afternoon before Easter, and Louise Everett was just preparing to start for the chapel, to help try the vestments on the boys of the new choir. She had lingered in the doorway for a moment to watch her brothers, who had gone on before her, laughing and shouting as they floundered along, now walking a few steps on top of the snow, now suddenly sinking down, up to the waist, as they chanced to find a spot where the chinook had done more rapid work. As she looked after them, she saw, crossing the road, one of the stray cows that wandered about the town. The ungainly animal came slowly along, turning this way and that, in search of a firmer footing, until all at once her hind legs plunged down into a hole, and the poor creature was left sitting bolt upright and staring stupidly about her, as if in astonishment at her unwonted position. Louise laughed at the absurd picture, but her heart failed her a little when she thought of the long walk in store for her.

"I've a great mind not to go," she said to herself; "the walking is so bad, and they don't really need me. I wish I'd sent the bundle down by the boys."

But she turned away and went to her room to put on her hat and jacket, for it was never her habit to fail to keep an engagement, and she had promised to be at the chapel that afternoon.

Perhaps it was the special providence supposed to watch over those who are doing their duty, perhaps it was because her light, quick steps made little impression on the snow; but more than two thirds of her walk was over, and the crust had not once given way beneath her. She was within sight of the chapel, now, but before she reached it, she must cross the small, open square, where the two main streets of the town came together. It was only fifteen or twenty yards, at most, but it lay lower than the ground about it, and the snow showed dark patches, here and there, as if the water had gathered below, and was trying to force its way to the surface. Louise glanced doubtfully at the square; but there was no other way she could take, and there were fresh footprints leading across it, showing that some one had been just before her. Moreover, she was late, and there was no time to be lost. With her skirts gathered closely about her, and the great bundle grasped in her other hand, she cautiously started forward, testing the ground at every step, before trusting her weight upon it. Slowly and carefully she went on, and was just congratulating herself upon her success, when--fwsch! There was a sound of crunching and gurgling, and her left foot plunged down through the snow, into six inches of water beneath, with a shock that threw the bundle from her hand, and jolted her hat over her eyes. With a smothered groan of mortification, she scrambled up to a solid footing once more, while she thrust back her hat, and gave a hasty glance over her shoulder, to assure herself that no one was in sight.

Not a human being was visible, except one man who was turning a distant corner. For so much, at least, she could be thankful. But it was plain that a further advance in that direction was impossible, and that she must beat a retreat. Accordingly, she picked up her bundle and turned to retrace her steps, moving with even greater caution than before, and stepping only in her previous tracks. However, the strain of one crossing was all that the weakened crust could bear, and the third step let her down again, far into the cold snow-water below, while her hat took a fresh lurch, this time to one side, and two or three hair-pins flew from her glossy yellow braids. Her situation was fast becoming tragic; but Louise gathered herself up anew and turned to the right, only to plunge in deeper than before; to the left, to meet with the same fate. Desperately she tried one spot after another. Now painfully scrambling to an insecure footing on top of the crust, now violently descending into the depths again, until the snow about her was marked thick with deep, round holes, and her feet were drenched and well-nigh frozen with the icy water which trickled up and down inside her shoes, as she lifted now her toes and now her heels from the horizontal.

"Pardon me, madam, but you seem to be in trouble. Can I assist you?" inquired a courteous voice behind her.

Slowly and painfully Louise turned around in her miniature well. Then she blushed to the roots of her hair. Ten feet away from her, on the outer edge of the square, stood a stranger, who was watching her with an air of respectful sympathy, which was entirely out of harmony with the amused twinkle of his gray eyes. One quick glance told the girl that the stranger was young and undeniably good-looking; then her eyes dropped to the bundle in her hand, as she answered,--

"Thank you, but I'm caught here, and can't seem to find a spot that will bear me. Don't trouble yourself; I shall get out in a moment. Oh, don't try to come here!" she added hastily, as he made a motion as if to go nearer her. "If you do, you will never get out."

The stranger paused doubtfully and looked at her again. There was a tone of good-breeding in her voice, and, as he came nearer, he saw that she was pretty, with a delicate, refined beauty which was not in keeping with her great bundle, her bedraggled appearance, and the hat cocked rakishly over one ear, above the drooping braids of yellow hair. At first sight, he had taken her for a pretty servant, out in search of a new place; but now he realized his mistake, and offered her a mental apology for his error.

"Perhaps I can tear a board or two off from that fence over there," he suggested, after a fresh survey of the field. "If you can stay there for a few minutes, I'll be back with some of them, and make a bridge."

In spite of herself, Louise laughed at the absurdity of her plight.

"Stay here!" she echoed; "I wish I could do anything else. But," she demurred, "I am afraid you will get into trouble, too."

But the stranger had already gone. A moment or two later, he was back again, with two long boards under his arm, as he picked his way along towards the young woman to whose rescue he had so valiantly devoted himself. Once back at his old station, he dropped one of the boards on the snow, pushed it towards her, tested its strength, and then walked the length of it, in order to place the other board in position. This second bridge brought him to her side.

"Now," he said gravely, as he bent forward and held out his hand, "let me take the bundle first."

Obeying him as implicitly as a child might have done, Louise handed him the great bundle the ragged corners of which bore unmistakable signs of her recent adventure, and he carefully conveyed it to a place of safety. Then he returned to the spot where she was standing in a sort of open pool, which was growing wider and deeper with her every motion.

"Please take hold of my hand," he said, with the same quiet courtesy which he might have shown in asking her for a waltz, though he pressed his lips firmly together, to keep back the smile which was trembling there. "Now, can you step up on the end of this board?"

For a moment Louise hesitated. The step was a long one, and, in her soaked condition, she had lost all her wonted elasticity of motion. However, something in the stranger's face made her feel that it was best for her to obey, with as few words as possible; so she mustered all her strength, made a violent effort, and scrambled up to the end of the board, striking it with a force which sent it swinging far to the left. For one instant she balanced herself upon her slippery foothold; then she fell backward with a suddenness that carried her rescuer with her, and they both plunged head foremost down into the gray pool below, just as Grant and Ned came out at the chapel door, to look for their missing sister.

As a general rule, there was but little observance of Sunday in Blue Creek. To the Eastern mind, it seemed strange to pass along the busy streets and see the carpenters hard at work upon a new house, or to listen to the clicking of the billiard balls in the wide-open rooms. In such a community, church-going was not a popular way of spending the time; but, on the next day, the little chapel was filled to overflowing with the throng that had gathered to hear the new choir. It was Easter evening, and the bright lights shone down on the masses of flowers on the altar and the white robes of the boys in the chancel, and on the closely-packed congregation below. Pipe organs and boy choirs were rare in the region, and the people of Blue Creek looked upon these as the means of furnishing an entertainment both novel and inexpensive; so it was to a large and varied audience that Mr. Nelson had the pleasure of preaching his Easter sermon. Aside from the regular attendants of the chapel, there were groups of rough miners alone and with their families, who were rarely to be found in any church; while, in the foremost rank, sat Wang Kum and a dozen intimate friends, their very pigtails waggling with suppressed excitement and admiration, as they looked about the pretty chancel and listened to the voices of the boys. Mr. Nelson's glance rested upon them for a moment, then passed on down the middle aisle, to one of the rear pews, where a stranger was standing, listening to the anthem with evident enjoyment.

He was a tall, well-built man of thirty, with bright brown hair and mustache, and his eyes showed large and gray when he raised them, now and then, as Charlie MacGregor's voice rang out above the rest of the choir. He appeared to be acquainted with no one there, for he had come in alone, and without making a sign of recognition to any one as he was ushered to his seat. Only twice had he seemed to be roused from his quiet repose of manner. When the first notes of the organ met his ear, he had glanced in that direction; and any one watching him closely might have seen him give a sudden start of surprise, while the color rose to his cheeks, as his eyes rested upon the organist. Once again, in the processional, he had started up with a quick smile of recognition, when he looked back at the advancing line of boys, and saw Charlie leading them; and he had bent towards the aisle to watch the lad, as he passed on, unconscious of the faces around him, in his happiness at once more being in his old place, at the head of a choir.

But the service was over, and the choir were coming towards him again, their voices ringing clear and high in the refrain of Le Jeune's *Jerusalem, the Golden*. Just as the leaders reached the stranger, there came a pause between the verses, and Charlie raised his eyes to meet the gray ones which were watching him so intently. Then his whole face brightened, and he smiled and nodded in glad recognition, as they went on down the aisle and out into the tiny choir-room.

The young man moved aside to let the other occupants of the pew pass out into the aisle; then he stepped back and waited, watching, meanwhile, the faces of the congregation, as they flocked past him. The group of Chinamen were lingering in front of the chancel, peering about at the lectern and font, and gazing up at the flower-laden altar.

"Heap nice; all samee Joss house," he heard one of them saying, with manifest approval.

Up in her corner beside the chancel, the organist was still playing her postlude; then she closed the organ, and rose to come down the steps, drawing on her gloves as she came. Before she had time to raise her eyes towards the congregation, the stranger was joined by Charlie MacGregor, who had hurried to the place where he was still pausing irresolutely, with his eyes fixed on Louise.

"Dr. Brownlee, when did you come?" the boy exclaimed, in enthusiastic welcome. "I didn't know you were here yet."

"I only came yesterday morning," the doctor answered, with a cordial smile which not only included Charlie, but extended to Howard and Ned who were lingering at a little distance, and casting curious glances at Charlie's unknown friend. "I was just in time to hear your new choir, but I never dreamed of finding you in it."

"Yes, I'm in it," returned Charlie, laughing. "I'm all at home here, now. I like it, too; ever so much-better than I thought I was going to. These are my cousin and his chums," he added, as they moved slowly down the aisle to where Grant had joined his brother and Howard. "And this," he went on, turning around abruptly, and speaking with the grace of manner so natural to him, "this is our organist, Miss Everett. Miss Lou, may I introduce Dr. Winthrop Brownlee, the friend I told you about meeting on the way out here?"

For a moment the doctor and Louise stared at each other, too much embarrassed to speak, while the color rushed to their faces. Then the doctor came to his senses, saying slowly,--

"I think I have met Miss Everett before."

And, to the utter mystification of the boys, they burst out laughing, and laughed as if they would never stop.

CHAPTER VI.

MARJORIE'S PARTY.

"O Allie," said Marjorie suddenly; "did you know that next Thursday is going to be mamma's birthday?"

"No, is it?" asked Allie, as she stooped to pick up the long, lean gray cat that was wandering aimlessly around them, and rubbing her hollow sides against their ankles. "I thought you gave Waif away, Marjorie."

"We did," responded Marjorie, laughing. "She was a stray cat that came to us, you know, and she was so homely that mamma didn't want her in the house, so we gave her to Dr. Hornblower, a month ago."

"Where'd she come from, then?" queried Allie, while she stroked the cat as she stood pawing and purring in her lap. "Wouldn't she stay with him?"

"Didn't I tell you? How queer, for we we've been laughing about it ever since! You see," Marjorie continued, "the doctor was lonesome, and wanted a cat for company, and we didn't want Waif, so we gave her to him. He was perfectly delighted with her, and carried her off home in a paper sack, with her head poking out through a hole in one side, and her tail sticking out the other. Two days later he stopped papa in the post-office and told him, 'Your kitty's caught a mouse.' The next week he met mamma and told her 'Kitty's caught three mice.' Then we didn't see anything more of him for ever so long, and we supposed that was the last of it; but, day before yesterday morning, he came to the door and handed a bundle to mamma, and said he didn't like the kitty as well as he thought he was going to, after all, so he'd brought her back. So here she is. Don't you want her?"

"I wouldn't take such a looking cat as a gift," returned Allie disdainfully. "But wasn't that just like Dr. Hornblower? He's very good; but he's as stupid as he can be, and I don't s'pose it ever occurred to him that he could pass the cat along to somebody else. Did you ever notice the way Mrs. Pennypoker always calls him 'good old Dr. Hornblower,' when she's ten years older than he is? I wonder how he'd like it, if he could hear her."

"I don't believe he'd mind, for he likes her so well; at least, he's there ever so much," said Marjorie innocently.

"H'm! you needn't think he goes to see Mrs. Pennypoker," said Allie scornfully.

"It's Miss Lou that he likes."

"Not that old man!" And Marjorie stared at her friend in amazement.

"He isn't so very old; and I don't know as I wonder if he does," replied Allie, with an air of great enjoyment in her small gossip. "I should think anybody might like Miss Lou, she's so pretty; and I just believe Mrs. Pennypoker is helping him on. You wait and see."

The two girls were sitting alone in the open front door of the Fishers' house, enjoying the late afternoon sun of a warm spring day. They had been off for a long ride with the boys, as was their frequent custom. The children all had their saddle ponies, and it was their delight to canter off, soon after lunch, for an hour or two among the pleasant mountain roads surrounding the town. On their return, they had stopped for a moment at Marjorie's door, to find that Mrs. Fisher had gone out to make some calls; and Marjorie had begged Allie to stay and keep her company until Allie had at length yielded and allowed the boys to go on without her.

There was a pause after Allie's last words; then Marjorie returned to her original charge.

"Yes," she resumed; "Thursday is going to be her birthday, and I want to celebrate. What can I do?"

"I don't know, I'm sure," answered Allie vaguely. "What do you want to do?"

"That's the worst of it," responded Marjorie thoughtfully. "I want it to be something that she'd like, and I don't know just what. I might--Let me see. I'll tell you," she added, with sudden inspiration, "I'll give her a surprise party."

"What?" And Allie looked at her friend, in astonishment at so daring a proposal.

"Yes, I'll give her a party," repeated Marjorie, nodding her head with decision.

"But do you suppose she'd like it?" inquired Allie dubiously.

"Of course she will. She 'most always has one for me on my birthday, you know," returned Marjorie; "and she wouldn't do that, if she didn't like them. She never had one herself; but that's only because she didn't have anybody to give her one."

Such logic was not to be resisted; and Allie felt her misgivings swept away while she listened.

"Besides," Marjorie went on enthusiastically; "I heard her say to papa, last night, that they'd take that very day to go over to Butte, and buy the new parlor carpet. They'll go in the morning early, and not come back till five, so that will just give us time, while they're out of the way. You'll help me get ready for it, won't you, Allie?"

"If mamma will let me," Allie was beginning, when Marjorie interrupted,--

"Your mother mustn't know anything about it; but we won't go to Mrs. Hammond that morning, we'll come here instead."

"I'm afraid we oughtn't to do that," remonstrated Allie feebly, although she was secretly longing to enter into the proposition.

"Why not?" demanded Marjorie. "Mamma gave up going to missionary meeting, last year, to get ready for my birthday party, and this is just the same thing. Don't be silly, Allie, but help me plan. I know mamma would say 'twas right," she added with an air of self-sacrificing virtue; "to give up our own improvement for the sake of making her happy."

"We might ask mamma," suggested Allie hopefully.

"Oh, no; she'd be sure to tell my mother, and that would spoil all the surprise," interposed Marjorie hastily. "It will be all right, I know. Would you have them come to supper, or just in the evening?"

"It's less work to have them come in the evening, isn't it?" asked Allie, losing her last doubts in the excitement of making plans for so momentous an occasion.

"Well, no," said Marjorie reflectively. "You have to feed them both times; and, in the evening, we'd have to have more salads and fancy things. We won't need so much, just for tea."

"What would you have?" inquired Allie, moving down to the lower step where her friend was sitting.

"Oh, just cake and preserves, and some kind of cold meat," returned Marjorie. "They'll be so busy talking they won't much mind what they get to eat, as long as there's plenty of it. We'll have it early, too, so they won't get so hungry. I can make splendid gingerbread, and the rest we can get down at the bakery; I haven't touched my this month's money yet. We'll work hard all the morning, and get the tables set and everything ready before mamma comes home, so they can be on hand to surprise her, when she comes in at the door."

"Yes," continued Allie, growing enthusiastic in her turn; "and then she won't need to have any care or worry about it; all she'll have to do will be just to sit in the parlor and make sure that they have a good time. At the table, she'll have to pour the tea; but we can pass things. Who're you going to invite?"

"Let's see," said Marjorie, pondering over the matter. "There's your father and mother, and Mr. Everett and Miss Lou and Mrs. Pennypoker; that's five."

"And Ned and Grant?" suggested Allie.

"Oh, no," answered Marjorie; "they'd only be in the way, and, besides, they're too young. This isn't a party for me, you know, and we can't have the boys."

"Not even Howard?" begged Allie. "He could help us cut meat, and wash dishes afterwards. He can do that as well as a girl."

"The boys can all come and wash dishes, after it's over, if they want to," returned Marjorie firmly; "but we can't have them at supper-time. I wouldn't mind Howard; but there's Charlie and the Everetts that would have to come, if he did, so we might as well stop before we begin. Where was I? Two Burnams and three Everetts and two Fishers, to start with: seven."

"And the Nelsons?" asked Allie.

"Yes, nine; and Dr. Hornblower is ten,--I suppose we ought to ask him,--and Mrs. Hammond is eleven, 'cause she might be cross next day, if we didn't invite her. And then that new doctor that Charlie knows--what is his name?"

"Dr. Brownlee?" inquired Allie. "But does your mother know him?"

"I don't think so," said Marjorie; "but he's real pleasant looking, and I've heard her say, ever so many times, that it's polite to welcome strangers when they first come to a place, so I know she'd want us to ask him. And then Miss Lou knows him a little bit, for I saw him take off his hat to her the other day; and she can introduce him. He makes twelve. I don't believe we'd better have any more. I'd like to ask Mr. Saunders, that keeps the fruit store down on the corner; but they say thirteen is unlucky, so perhaps twelve will do."

"All right," agreed Allie. "How are you going to ask them?"

"I shall just say, 'Mamma wishes you'd come to supper at half past five.' I won't ask them till the night before for fear somebody'd tell her; but if she goes on the early train, it will be safe enough."

"Then aren't you going to say it's a surprise party?" asked Allie, rising to go home, as she saw Mrs. Fisher coming up the street.

"No; for I'm afraid they mightn't come," said Marjorie, in a low voice. "Now, Allie, don't you dare to breathe a word of this to anybody, not even to Howard, for I want it to be a perfect surprise. And you know you've promised to help me out in the morning."

Five days later, two flushed and grimy, but triumphant young hostesses stood gazing at the tables before them. Marjorie's plan had been carried into effect; and her guests, one and all, had gratefully accepted Mrs. Fisher's invitation to tea, for they knew of old that her little parties were the most enjoyable ones in the camp. Even Dr. Brownlee had sent a cordial message of acceptance, for though he was surprised at the invitation, coming as it did from a stranger whom he did not even know by sight, he attributed it to the proverbial Western hospitality, and was glad of anything which could bring him into connection with the people among whom he was to live. Early that morning Mr. and Mrs. Fisher had gone away for a long, tedious day of shopping, and an hour later Allie and Marjorie had invaded the kitchen for four hours of hard work. By noon all was in readiness, and they could pause to contemplate the result of their labors.

The table was stretched to its utmost length, and bright with snowy linen and glass and silver, while around it were gathered twelve chairs, taken from the different rooms, in order to accommodate the unusual number of guests. Here a dining-room chair stood beside one borrowed from Mrs. Fisher's bedroom; there kitchen wood and parlor upholstery were placed side by side, in striking contrast. The table itself was groaning beneath the weight of the feast, for Marjorie had been liberal in her selection from her mother's preserves; while a whole boiled ham, fresh from the bakehouse, stood before Mr. Fisher's place, and at the other end of the table his wife's chair was decked with ribbons, and confronted with a great loaf of cake, whose uneven icing bore, in red sugar, the letters "M.C.F.," traced by an inexperienced hand. This was Allie's contribution to the banquet, and Marjorie had thoughtfully surrounded it with a circle of thirty-nine tiny candles, which stood ready for the lighting. Plates of assorted cookies were scattered about the board; here lay a low dish of olives, whose dusky green contrasted well with the ruddy globe of an Edam cheese, placed beside them, and there rose a towering pyramid of golden oranges flanked on either side by a tempting pile of purple and white grapes.

"It does look pretty, doesn't it, Allie?" asked Marjorie for the fifth time.

"Yes," said Allie, as she bent forward to break a corner off from one of the cookies and tuck it into her mouth. "Yes, it is lovely. I do hope your mother will like it. But now I must hurry, or mamma will know something is going to happen."

"Go on, then; only be sure you're back here by five," Marjorie warned her. "And don't let the boys come here this afternoon, for I'm too tired to even look at them."

At half past five, the guests had assembled and were sitting in the parlor, looking a little annoyed and uncomfortable as the moments passed by and their hostess did not appear.

"Come right in," Marjorie had said to them, one after another; "Mamma will be so glad to see you; she'll be here in a minute."

Last of all came Dr. Brownlee. He had been delayed until the last possible moment, and now, just as Mr. and Mrs. Fisher turned the corner far down the street, he rang at the door, to be admitted by Marjorie. Once inside the parlor, he stopped and looked around the room in search of his hostess, in order to offer her a prompt apology for his seeming rudeness in being so late. To his surprise, there was no one present at all answering to the description of Mrs. Fisher which he had received from his landlady.

"Hamlet, without the ghost!" he thought to himself, as he paused irresolutely, just across the threshold, and glanced about in vain for a familiar face.

For a moment there was an awkward hush. Most of the guests knew the doctor by sight, but in the explicable absence of their hostess, no one was sufficiently at ease to rise and bid the stranger welcome to another person's house. They tried to go on with their conversation, in apparent unconsciousness of the young man who stood in the doorway, reddening under their sidelong glances; but their attempt was not crowned with success, and there came one of those seemingly interminable pauses which sometimes fall upon a room. Then, all at once, Louise Everett rose from her chair in the bay-window, where she had been hidden behind the ample shoulder of Mrs. Pennypoker, and, crossing the room, she greeted the doctor as an old acquaintance. A few words passed between them; then she introduced him to the other guests, before leading the way back to her own cosy corner, where Mrs. Burnam sat waiting to welcome him, as the friend of her young nephew.

"Who's that going in at our house?" Mr. Fisher had asked, peering over the top of the pile of bundles in his arms. "It looks like Dr. Brownlee; but why should he be going there?"

"Oh, dear; I hope it isn't anybody coming to call," sighed his wife, with the inhospitality born of a long day of tedious, unsatisfactory shopping. But she quickened her pace, in order to discover who was the guest awaiting them.

At the door she was met by Marjorie, dressed in her best gown, and looking strangely excited.

"Let me take your things, mamma," she said in a low tone. "There's somebody to see you in the parlor."

Forcing a smile to her tired face, Mrs. Fisher advanced to the door to greet her caller. On the threshold she paused aghast, for, to her startled eyes, the room appeared to be thronged with people, who rose and stepped forward to meet her, while Marjorie stood at her side, gleefully clapping her hands and exclaiming,--

"It's a surprise party, mamma! It's a surprise party!"

For one instant, Mrs. Fisher faltered. She had come home in a state of utter exhaustion, and she longed to run away from the parlor and hide. But the next minute her courage came back to her, in the face of her roomful of guests, and she gave them as hearty a welcome as if the party had been one of her own making. Up and down the room she went, speaking a word here, shaking a hand there, all with the tact for which her hospitality was noted. She had sent one appealing glance towards Louise, and the girl, taking in the situation in a moment, had come to her aid, with Dr. Brownlee at her side. In a short time the room was buzzing with voices, as the guests entered into the full tide of conversation.

Suddenly the dining-room door swung open, and Allie appeared on the threshold.

"Please come out to supper, now," she said shyly, as she met her mother's surprised glance.

There was another pause of uncertainty; then Mr. Everett offered his arm to Mrs. Fisher, and led the way to the table, where the guests seated themselves as they wished, gazing, meanwhile, with amused eyes at the feast before them. A short silence followed, and then the conversation started up once more, as Mr. Fisher, with one despairing glance at his wife, attacked the vast ham before him, and Mrs. Fisher began to pour out the pale, watery effusion which filled the teapot. Allie and Marjorie were already bestirring themselves to pass the plates and cups about the table; but all at once Marjorie paused abruptly, with her arm outstretched, as she gazed blankly this way and that. Then her face grew red and the sudden tears rushed to her eyes, as she hurried out of the room, with a gesture to Allie to follow her.

"What is it, Marjorie?" Allie exclaimed in alarm, as the young hostess sank down into the wood box and buried her face in her hands.

An inarticulate moan was her only answer.

"Marjorie! Marjorie!" she urged again. "Tell me what's the matter. Are you ill?"

Then Marjorie raised her head for a moment.

"I'm all right," she said, with a great sob of shame; "but what shall we do, Allie? We ate up all the bread for breakfast, and I forgot to order any more."

It was late that evening when the guests took their leave; and, as they went away down the street together, they said, over and over again, that Mrs. Fisher had never before been half so bright and witty in her talk, so quick to plan new modes of entertainment. Their hostess watched them out of sight; then, after an expressive look at her husband, she turned away from the door, and crossed the hall to Marjorie's room. All was dark within, as she opened the door and entered; but, as soon as her eyes had grown accustomed to the gloom, she went up to the bed, and laid her hand on a small, dark body, curled up on the white spread.

"Marjorie, dear," she said gently.

The childish figure was quivering with suppressed sobs; but there was no other answer.

"Marjorie," she said again; "don't feel so badly about it, my child."

The tone of motherly sympathy was too much for Marjorie's self-control, and the tears began to come, thick and fast.

"O mamma," she cried; "truly we didn't mean to. I'm so sorry."

Mrs. Fisher sat down on the side of the bed, and drew her daughter towards her.

"Don't cry so, Marjorie," she repeated. "I know you didn't mean to do anything out of the way. Tell me how you came to ask all these people here."

Between her sobs, Marjorie told her mother the whole story; and Mrs. Fisher rejoiced that the kindly darkness hid her smile, as she listened to her little daughter's incoherent explanation of the party and its cause.

"And I meant it should all be so nice," Marjorie ended, with a fresh burst of tears; "and it was just dreadful. I forgot the bread, and the candles wouldn't burn, and nobody knew Dr. Brownlee, and everything was horrid. Scold me, if you want to; but I truly meant to give you a good time, only it all went wrong."

"Marjorie, dear," her mother said, when she could steady her voice enough to speak; "I know you meant to make me have a happy birthday, and I am grateful to my little girl for taking so much pains for me. Another time we will talk it over together, and plan the best thing to do, instead of your trying to surprise me. And now forget all about the worry of it, and only remember that you've done what you could to make the day pleasant for me." And she bent over for a goodnight kiss, before she returned to the kitchen for a long hour of dish-washing and putting the room to rights.

CHAPTER VII.

JANEY'S PROPHECY.

"Git up in de mawnin' singin', an' de cat cotch you befo' night," Janey had said oracularly, when Allie ran out into the kitchen, that morning before breakfast, with the refrain of one of Charlie's songs upon her lips.

"What nonsense, Janey!" said Allie, laughing at the strange, old-time saying. "I don't believe the cat'll 'cotch' me any more for singing, and it's ever so much more fun than 'tis to cry."

In fact, there was no particular reason that Allie should not sing, for life looked very attractive to her that morning. The bright June sunshine was lying warm over the town, and giving back a dazzling lustre from the snow-capped mountains which rose up from the midst of the summer landscape; lessons were over for the present, and, best of all, Mr. and Mrs. Burnam were to go out to camp that day, to make final arrangements for the long-talked-of week, when the Everetts, Burnams, and Fishers were to pitch their tents beside the engineering camp, in the Bitter Root Mountains, and enjoy a week of roughing it in the wilderness. Soon after breakfast they drove away from the door, with Victor snugly tucked in between them, while Allie, with the boys and Ben, stood on the piazza, to wave them a good-by. The children lingered there until the wagon was out of sight; then they turned back into the house, feeling very important over the prospect of two days of housekeeping on their own account.

But, after all their anticipations, the morning did not prove to be quite as enjoyable as they had hoped it would be. Marjorie had been invited to spend the day with them; but, unfortunately, Marjorie was in one of her perverse fits, and so successfully devoted herself to the task of being disagreeable that Allie was at her wits' end how to manage her; Howard openly quarrelled with her, and even Charlie, the courteous, marched out of the room and slammed the door behind him, while he sang, with tantalizing distinctness,--

"'Oh, jimineddy! And oh, goody gracious! How I did love her! But she was contumacious.'"

This last insult was too much for Marjorie to bear, for, in her secret heart, she greatly admired Charlie, and longed to have him for her ally and champion, instead of being forced to watch his unswerving devotion to his cousin. As the door closed behind him, she flew after him, to deliver herself of one parting shot,--

"Charlie MacGregor, I de-test you! You're no gentleman, even if you do think you are; and I only hope you'll get what you deserve for being so rude to me, when I'm company."

Then the door banged again with even greater violence than before, and Marjorie burst out crying, as she put on her hat and departed, without a word to Allie.

Her irate guest once gone, Allie moved up and down the rooms, putting them in order with much the same dazed feeling as that which comes in the sudden hush that sometimes follows a violent thunder-shower. The more she pondered on the events of the morning, she could not see that either she herself or the two boys were in any way to blame for Marjorie's explosion, and as she forlornly sat down to the lunch table, she felt as if she were in part realizing the truth of Janey's prediction. However, she was too much accustomed to Marjorie's sudden fits of temper, and too well acquainted with her really kind heart, to dwell long upon the matter; so before the meal was ended she was gayly laughing with the boys, and planning for the next day's frolic.

"Come out and have a ride, Allie," urged Charlie, as they left the table. "I have a kind of a sort of a feeling that I'm in disgrace, and I want some fun to console me."

Allie laughed.

"How silly you are to mind what Marjorie says!" she answered. "She'll be all over it by to-morrow, and like you better than ever; I know just how angelic she always is, after one of these times. But if you want a ride, I'll be ready in an hour. I've promised to write a letter for Janey, first."

"To his Goatship?" inquired Howard disrespectfully. "All right; we'll go out and play ball till time to get the ponies." And they went away, while Allie stood in the door, saucily calling after them to be good boys and not get into mischief.

"Now, Janey," she said, as she went out into the kitchen; "I'll write that letter for you before you wash the dishes or anything; because Mr. Charlie wants me to go to ride with him, as soon as I can." And she seated herself at the table, while Janey went after her writing materials.

"How you done like my paper, Miss Allie?" the girl asked proudly, as she laid upon the table a sheet of vivid, rose-colored paper, and its accompanying envelope, which brought with them an aggressive fragrance of musk. Then she dropped down on the floor behind her young mistress, coiling herself up in the corner, with her back against the wall, that she might dictate at her ease.

"My dear frien'," she began slowly, and with the air of searching her mind for properly sonorous phrases; "I have done receive your letter, an' I take my pen in han' to now reply. I was very glad to know dat you is well, an' I am sorry to say I am not; I think I have de consumption"--

"Why, Janey," interposed Allie; "what do you mean? Aren't you well?"

"Yes, I's well enough," answered Janey, as she shot a sudden mischievous glance from the corners of her downcast eyes; "but I reckon he'll think more of me, ef he thinks I's goin' to die. I am not very happy," she resumed, in the same stilted tone as before; "an' las' night you came to me in a dream, an' tol' me you was dead. I done specks he'll cry like everything, when he reads dat," she interpolated, with a nod of triumph. "Sometimes I reckon we sha'n' never see each other no mo'; but you mus' never forget your Janey. Um-mm," she went on, in an inarticulate mumble.

"What?" inquired Allie, pausing, with her pen in mid air, as she turned around to see Janey with her cap off, a row of hair-pins between her lips, and a pair of gleaming scissors raised to one of her woolly tails.

There was a sudden sound of snipping steel, and then Janey continued,--

"I sen' you a plat of my hair, an' I wants you to sen' me one of yours; an'--an--'" Janey hesitated, while she put on her cap once more.

"Well, what next?" asked Allie, secretly wondering, as she glanced at the sable tress before her, why each could not retain his own hair, since the two locks would probably be so much alike that only the keen eye of an expert or a lover could distinguish between them.

"So no mo' now," dictated Janey. "Give my love to Emma Digson, an' Joe Harrison, an' my mother, an' tell little Bill he mus' be a good boy, an' tell Sarah Johnson"--Here followed a list of greetings and messages, as long as those at the end of the Pauline epistles.

Allie was still toiling her way through them, making conscientious attempts to discover the proper spelling of names, when she heard the front door open and shut. A moment later, Howard appeared in the kitchen, very pale and with trembling lips.

"Come here a minute, Allie," he said, in a tone of command so unlike his usual manner that his sister started up at the first word.

"What is it?" she demanded hastily. "What do you want of me?"

But Howard had already hurried back to the parlor. She followed him, with a dull, cold feeling about her heart, as she became more and more convinced that there was some trouble. As she reached the parlor door, she drew back, for a moment, in alarm. On the sofa lay Charlie, with his handkerchief tied over the upper part of his face, and his cheeks and lips as white as Howard's had been. The next instant she sprang forward to his side, crying,--

"O Charlie, what has happened? Are you hurt? What is it?"

With a strong effort, the boy steadied his voice enough to say quietly, as he stretched out his hand towards the spot where he had heard her drop down on her knees beside the sofa,--

"'Tisn't much, Allie; so don't get rattled. Howard'll tell you about it." And he paused abruptly, biting his lip to keep from crying out with pain.

"We were playing ball, and Charlie went to catch. He muffed, somehow, and the ball hit him in the eye; it smashed his glasses, and they've cut his eyes some," explained Howard, in a hurried, breathless tone, while he tramped nervously up and down the room.

"What can we do? If mamma were only here, Howard! Is it very bad, Charlie?" And for a moment Allie's head dropped beside her cousin's, while she shook with sobs of mingled pity and fear. Then she started up again, to force back her tears as she said, with all the pride and energy of the MacGregors in her firm, clear voice,--

"Howard, don't rush round so; you'll only make Charlie worse. It may not be so bad; but you go, quick as you can, for Dr. Brownlee. Run every single step of the way, and don't you come back without him."

For an instant, Howard stared admiringly at the determined little figure before him; then he rushed away, glad to get out of sight, where he could rub the tears off from his cheeks, and feeling an immediate relief in the need for prompt action. Twenty minutes later he came back, accompanied by the doctor, whom he had met on the street, not far from his office.

As Allie rose from her place beside the sofa, she was filled with a momentary dislike of this handsome, well-dressed young man, with the red carnation in his button-hole, who came into the room with a sort of quiet briskness, and addressed a half-laughing remark of greeting to Charlie. But as she watched him, she soon realized that there was nothing unsympathetic in his cheerfulness; and she felt a quick trust in him, when she looked up into his kind gray eyes, while he bent over Charlie and took the handkerchief from his face. An older person would have read much from the sudden frown which passed across his forehead; but Allie failed to catch it, and was cheered by his next words,----

"Only a scratch or two, and a little cut. We'll patch you up soon, my boy, so you needn't worry. There's a little glass left here, though, that we want to get out of the way, first of all. You say your parents are away?" he asked, turning to Allie. "Do you suppose you can help me a little; or are you afraid?"

Allie's cheeks grew white at the thought; and the doctor, as he watched her, added kindly,--

"Or perhaps your brother"--

But Howard had fled, to shut himself up in his mother's room. Allie could hear him moving restlessly about, behind the closed door.

"I'll help if I can," she said bravely, though her rigid lips would scarcely form the words; and she dropped her hand on Charlie's cold fingers, to feel them close around it, with a grateful pressure, as the doctor said approvingly,--

"That's a brave girl! Now, has your mother anything that I could use for bandages?"

Allie hurried away in search of the great "emergency basket," which her mother always kept well stocked with rolls of old cotton and linen and flannel. The doctor gave a quick nod of pleasure, as he saw the orderly store.

"Good!" he said, as if to himself; "that tells the story. I wish more women would look out for such things. Now," he went on, while he drew a chair to the window, and laid a little case of shining, ugly-looking instruments on a table beside it; "we must get rid of that glass as soon as we can; and I want you, little woman, to hold this boy's head tight, very tight, so he can't move, no matter how much I do hurt him. Any slip now would be very serious."

There followed a short interval of silence, when Charlie ground his teeth hard together, to keep back any sound, and Allie sturdily held her place at the back of his chair, though she felt faint and sick at the sight before her, as those horrible little steel points moved up and down across her cousin's eye. Then the doctor spoke again, in his cheery, pleasant way, while he adjusted the necessary bandages; but to Allie his voice sounded a long way off, and she dropped to the floor in a forlorn little heap, as soon as she received the doctor's nod to assure her that her work was ended.

"You're a plucky pair," said Dr. Brownlee then, as he led the boy back to the sofa, and arranged a pillow under his head. "I don't know which has been braver, but I'm proud of you both. The worst is over now; but we want to get this boy into bed, where he can keep quiet for a day or two. I wish we could send word to your mother; but I suppose that is out of the question, so we shall have to get along without her. Still, you've a good nurse here, Charlie," he added, with an admiring glance at Allie, who had roused herself once more and was standing by the sofa, with one slender hand resting on her cousin's forehead.

"Shall I get his room ready?" she asked, as her blue eyes filled with tears again; for the doctor's kind words were too much for her shaken nerves to bear.

"Yes, he'll be better there," the doctor answered, as he followed her into the room which the two boys usually occupied. "A southwest corner room," he said, glancing around it. "That's too strong a light; isn't there somewhere else?"

"Mine is on the other side," she suggested.

"That's better; but what will you do, my young nurse?" he asked with the gentle courtesy which was habitual with him.

"I'll take the sofa, or anywhere," she said, as she led the way into her own dainty little room. "He can have this to himself, too; and Howard is in the other. I truly don't mind a bit being turned out." She paused and glanced over her shoulder to make sure that the door was shut. "Is it very bad, Dr. Brownlee?" she asked, in a frightened whisper.

"I can't tell yet; but I hope not," the doctor said reassuringly. "Now, little woman, listen to me. Your cousin will have to be shut up here in the dark for a good many days, and your mother will be away till to-morrow night. I might send for somebody to come and stay with you; but it would only frighten Charlie, so I am going to leave him in your care, instead. You've just been doing splendidly with him; and he's used to you, and likes to have you round him. Now, do you suppose you can see to him till bedtime, and through the day to-morrow? A great deal, much more than you know, depends on his being kept quiet and content, without any worry. I will come back this evening, and sleep on the sofa here, where I can look out for him through the night. Do you think you can do it?"

"I will," answered Allie, as solemnly as if she had been taking her marriage vows.

The doctor studied her face intently. Such a little thing, a happy, rollicking child! But, in the past hour, she had shown herself a woman, in the courage and tenderness which her love for her cousin had given her. He felt that he could trust her, even in such a critical case as this. But, as he looked down at the wistful, white face, and the drawn lips which yet made no complaint of weakness or of fear, some sudden impulse made him stoop and lift her hand to his lips.

"I am glad to bend the knee before so brave and true a lady," he said, with assumed lightness to mask his real feeling. "I hope the time may come when I shall be able to prove how gladly I would serve her."

"Cure Charlie's eye, then," she answered, with quaint, serious directness.

"My dear little girl, I will if I can," he replied gravely.

Then he turned away, to close the blinds, draw down the shades, and pull together the heavy curtains, until the room lay in deep shadow. At sight of these ominous preparations, Allie's fear came back to her.

"Oh, must he stay like this, all in the dark?" she cried, in a sudden terror of she knew not what.

"For a little while," answered the doctor, his voice sounding brisk and cheery again, through the thick darkness. "We'll try not to have it last any longer than we can help. Now," he went on kindly, "if you'll go out in the sunshine and take a little run, while you get quieted down, I'll help Charlie into bed. Then I shall leave him in your hands."

But Allie was in no mood for sunshine. She paused for one moment beside her cousin, without daring to trust her voice to speak; then she fled to the kitchen, and cast herself into Janey's arms, to cry as if her young heart were breaking.

"Miss Allie, honey," Janey begged her; "what is it? Tell Janey what's de matter.

Don' cry so, Miss Allie, don't."

Allie was past heeding her words. It had taken all her courage and self-control to go through the last hour, and, now that she could have a moment to herself, she could only cling to Janey and sob with a bitterness which brought the sympathetic tears into the dark eyes above her.

"What is it, honey?" asked Janey again, as the child grew more quiet.

"Oh, Janey, it's Mr. Charlie!" And Allie's head went over against the girl's shoulder once more.

Janey looked pityingly down into the swollen, flushed face before her. Then she seated herself in a chair, and gathering up the child in her strong, young arms, she rocked gently to and fro without speaking, while Allie sobbed out the story of the accident. When she paused, the girl's brown cheek lay, for a moment, against the soft, thick hair, in an unspoken caress; then she said cheerfully,--

"Now, Miss Allie, dear, it's too bad, and Janey's sorry for you all. But jus' you dry up your eyes, an' don' cry no mo'. Mars' Charlie's too good a boy for de Lord to give him very bad time, an' 'twon't be long befo' he's all right again. Janey's awful sorry for you; but you jus' try to keep jolly, for his 'count, an' your ma will be home to-morrow. It'll all come out for de bes'," she added, with the simple faith of her people, which somehow comforted Allie, and gave her new strength to go on.

A few minutes later, the doctor sent Howard in search of his sister, and Allie was able to go quietly back into her room. It looked strangely unfamiliar to her; but as her eyes became accustomed to the darkness, she gradually made out the figure of her cousin, who was lying in her dainty bed, with broad white bandages covering his eyes.

"Is that you, Allie?" he asked eagerly, as the door opened. "The doctor says you're to look out for me to-day, and I'm no end glad of it."

"Yes," said the doctor, from his corner where Allie had not yet seen him; "you couldn't have a better nurse. Now," he added, after giving her a few simple directions, "I shall be back early this evening, and, till then, you're in charge. All you have to do," he went on, as Allie followed him to the door, "is to wait on him, and see that the light doesn't get to him. You can talk to him, just as you always do, only be a little quiet. Above all, don't let him get to thinking about his eye, for he mustn't worry. Good-by."

He left her to go back into her cousin's room, while he went down the street, saying to himself,--

"I wish I could often get as plucky a patient and nurse. But I'd give a good deal if I had a first-class oculist in town to-night; I don't like the looks, up there."

CHAPTER VIII.

IN THE DARK.

Often and often, during the next few weeks, Allie recalled the conversation which had taken place between herself and Marjorie, months before; for Charlie's time had come to prove his ability to bear trouble and suffering as bravely as a boy could do. Early on the afternoon following the accident, Dr. Brownlee had saddled his horse and ridden away to meet Mrs. Burnam, and prepare her for the new care awaiting her; but it was not until the next day that he told her of his real fear, the danger that the injured eye might become so seriously inflamed that its sight would be destroyed. How Howard and Allie found it out, it would be impossible to say; but, before the day was over, they knew the secret, and hovered about their cousin with an anxious care, the real cause of which he understood as little as he did that of the doctor's extreme gentleness of voice and touch, when he came, morning and night, to examine the wound and renew the bandages.

It was a hard experience for the boy, for there were long days of sickening, throbbing pain, that darted up and down about his eye, and painted strange, lurid pictures against the darkness of his closed lids. Then came the time when he was allowed to sit up once more, and to wander clumsily about his narrow quarters, bruising himself by frequent collisions with the unseen furniture, until Allie's heart ached for him, and she longed to tear away the bandages, and let him have one short hour of daylight again. His piano was his main solace in these days, for Mrs. Burnam had had it moved into his room, and he amused himself with it for long hours at a time, when his cousins were busy, or away from home. Of course he grumbled a little at times, as any healthy boy would do; of course he had hours of being undeniably cross; but, for the most part, he showed a quiet endurance which won the admiration of all his friends.

But, little by little, as the danger passed, his privileges increased, and he was free to make daily excursions out into the parlor, which was darkened for his use, and to receive short calls from the Everetts and Marjorie. Allie had been his constant companion in these weeks, entertaining him, leading him about the room, and even feeding him the meals which Mrs. Burnam and Janey prepared so daintily. Then, at length, came the great day when the bandage was taken off, to be replaced by a shade, and only resumed for the hour when Allie was to be allowed to lead him up and down the sunny piazza, and out along the street for daily-increasing distances. For Charlie, all this was like coming back into life once more. In spite of the darkness of his room, he could yet see the dim outlines of objects in his narrow line of vision, and grope his way about without being dependent upon his cousins for his every need; and after a month of perfect helplessness, even this was a relief, and he accepted it gratefully.

And, after all, dark as the days were, they yet had their bright spots. In his constant visits, the doctor had quite won Charlie's heart with his lively talk and fun, until the boy found himself eagerly looking forward to the next call, and wondering what fresh interest his new friend had in store for him. For the doctor, true to the instincts of his profession, knew so well how to cover his real anxiety under his gay, light manner, that his young patient had no idea of the possible danger of his case, and only regarded it as a tedious, painful wound which would soon heal.

"I am getting most awfully sick of this, though," he said one day, after the doctor had gone. "It's a shame to be losing all this jolly weather, and I've forgotten how everything looks. Dr. Brownlee is a first-rate man; but he needn't make such a fuss over a scratch. I say, Allie, let's run away and go for a ride up the gulch."

"Oh, wouldn't I like to!" responded Allie, with a fervor which led Charlie to say gratefully,--

"I'll tell you what, Allie; it's a shame for you to stay tucked up with me in this hole. You've stuck by me like a Trojan; but I'm well enough off alone. Go out and have a lark; I would if I could."

"Sha'n't!" returned Allie composedly. "Besides, there isn't anybody to lark with."

"Where are Marjorie and the boys?" demanded Charlie, casting himself down in the easy-chair, and turning to face Allie, as she stood leaning against the window curtain.

"They went fishing with Mr. Everett, up the cañon."

"Bother!" exclaimed Charlie impatiently. "Here I am losing all the fun; and you're so silly, you won't go without me, when you could, as well as not. That's just like a girl."

"Now, Charlie, you just keep your temper," said Allie laughingly, while she covered his mouth with her hand. "If you say anything more that's saucy, I'll go off and never come back. I didn't want to go to-day; it's too warm. Besides, we'll make up for all this when we go into camp."

"Are we really going? I thought 'twas given up." And Charlie started up with quick enthusiasm.

"Yes, the plans are all made, and we're only waiting for you to be able to go. We're going to be gone two weeks, and"--Allie paused, before imparting her final bit of good news--"papa has asked Dr. Brownlee to go too."

"How jolly!" Charlie exclaimed rapturously.

"Isn't it? The doctor didn't want you to get where he couldn't see to you; and we all like him so much that papa said this was the best thing to do, so we're going to start the very first day you are able."

"When does he say 'twill be?" asked the boy eagerly.

Allie hesitated. This part of her news was not so pleasant, for since the first danger was over and Charlie was allowed to be up and about the room, she knew that he was restless, and longing to be out with the boys, enjoying his old free life once more.

"Well," he urged again, "when can we go?"

"Not for three or four weeks," she said gently, as her hand fell down from his face, and rested on his shoulder with a little caressing gesture.

The boy needed all her sympathy, for his disappointment was keen. The prospect of a month more of an existence like that of the past three weeks was too much for his courage; and, shaking off her hand, he rose and tramped up and down the room, frowning and moody.

"I won't stand it!" he exclaimed suddenly, as he paused. "There's no need of it, Allie, and I'm just not going to stand another month of it. I'll risk my eyes, or let them slide; but I must get out of this stuffy old room inside of a week, or I'll know the reason why."

But his temper was always short-lived, and he was soon his old bright self again. That night he was cheered by hearing the doctor say that he might go out into the parlor to see Ned and Grant for an hour in the morning.

From that time on, his days began to pass more quickly. With Ned and Marjorie at their head, the young people showed unlimited patience and ingenuity in planning new amusements for their friend; and not a day passed that they did not descend upon him in a body, laden with offerings of fruit and flowers, trophies of their fishing expeditions, and bits of gay gossip from mine and smelter, choir and Chinatown.

Marjorie, in particular, was his devoted slave. For the past few weeks, she had been carrying, deep down in her heart, a little sore spot, left there by the stinging memory of her hasty words an hour before the accident; and, now that she could see her friend once more, she did her best to make amends for her past sins. But though her endless fun and rollicking kindness gave Charlie many a pleasant hour, it was to Allie that he turned in any emergency, for her long days of devotion to him had proved her a staunch, true friend.

"Allie is a pretty good sort of girl," he confided to Ned one day. "She's just the kind to have round when you aren't well, for she's jolly, and takes first-rate care of you, without being soft."

One afternoon, about three or four weeks after the accident, Marjorie and the three boys were sitting on the little front porch at the Everetts', reposing after a long ride. It was a cool, cloudy day; the mist lay low over the mountain sides, and closed in between the walls of the cañon, and the wind blew up fresh and sharp. Allie had watched the little group of riders as they cantered past the house and, turning the corner, stopped at the Everetts'. Then she was seized with a sudden inspiration.

"Get up, lazy boy," she commanded, going into her room where Charlie lay on the sofa, stretched out at his ease, with his arms folded under his head. "Mamma's coming in here, in a minute, to put on your blinders, and then let's go down to the Everetts' for an hour. They're all down there, and we'll take them by surprise."

Charlie started up eagerly enough. It was the longest walk that he had taken, and he was glad to get out of his dull routine; so, ten minutes later, he was on his way, with his hat pulled down over his face to cover the ignominious bandage, and Allie's hand on his arm.

Grant was the first to see him coming.

"Hurrah!" he shouted. "There's Charlie Mac!"

"Where?" exclaimed Ned, turning around with a suddenness which made him lose his balance, as he sat on the rail, and sent him rolling over backwards to the ground. He was on his feet again in a twinkling, and tore away up the street to meet his guest, and, usurping Allie's place as escort, bring him back to the steps in triumph. "Sit down here, old fellow," he said, as he deposited him in a chair, and seated himself protectingly on the arm. "How jolly to have you round again!"

"Glad you think so," responded Charlie; "I was feeling fine to-day, and Allie thought 't would be a good scheme to come down here. You can just believe I was ready for a change of base."

The first chatter of eager greeting was not yet ended, when Louise Everett appeared in the doorway behind them.

"I must just come out to speak to Charlie," she said, as she stepped forward to his chair. "It's so long since I've seen you. No, don't get up," she added hastily; "you look too comfortable to let me disturb you, so I'll just sit down on the step beside Howard, if there's room."

"Always room for you, Miss Lou," returned Howard gallantly, as he curled up his feet so that his dusty shoes should not soil her fresh, pink gown. "We've set Charlie up in the middle, like a Chinese idol, and are adoring him."

"You'd better get Wang Kum out here to help," suggested the idol complacently. "I'm afraid I'm not much to look at, Miss Lou; but fortunately I don't have to see myself these days. I leave it to Allie, to tell me if my hair's smooth."

Louise laughed, as she rested one hand affectionately on the girl's shoulder.

"The doctor says she has been a most devoted Allie; and we all think that we haven't seen much more of her than of you, this last month."

"I know that, Howard and I aren't any account, any longer," said Marjorie, in an injured tone, from her seat on the rail. "Howard, which of us shall get broken to pieces, so the other can 'tend to it?"

"What's the use?" returned Howard languidly. "Our noses are out of joint now, and it doesn't seem to do us any good."

"Oh, by thunder!" exclaimed Grant, suddenly.

"Grant, dear, what words!" said his sister reprovingly.

"Can't help it, Lou; look there! Dr. Hornblower is coming down the road, and I can see, by the northeast corner of his weather eye, that he's going to stop and make us a visit."

"Dr. Hornblower? Do put me out of sight somewhere," begged Charlie.

"What for? You've never seen him, and he's lots of fun," said Howard, without the faintest appearance of respect for the clerical brother.

"I know, but I'd rather meet him some time when I don't feel so much like a mummy in a museum," urged Charlie again. "Can't you get me out of this, Ned?"

"There isn't time, honestly. He's right here, or I would," answered Ned in a low voice, as he drew his friend's soft hat forward and turned down the brim. "You're all right; and, besides, he's such an old duffer that he won't notice anything. He won't stay here, any way; he comes to see cousin Euphemia, and help her out when she gets in a tight place with Wang Kum. Wang's been cutting church lately, and most likely the doctor's come to see about it."

The Reverend Gabriel Hornblower belonged to the fast vanishing school of mossbacks, or "old-timers," as they more elegantly termed themselves, the early settlers who had watched the State grow from its first squatter population to its present comparative civilization. A mere boy in the stormy days of Sixty-three, he had joined one of the many trains of ox-teams which started across the country, on their slow, toilsome march to the far West; and, for the next few years, his life had been one of continual excitement and hardship. His father and grandfather before him had been ministers; so it was small wonder that Gabriel, upon arriving at man's estate, should feel that both his family tradition and his name had called him to the life of a wandering preacher among the mining camps and scattered ranches of the region, until he had finally settled down to take charge of the little church in Blue Creek. He was neither a great man, nor an educated one. On the contrary, he was ignorant of any life outside of his own narrow sphere, and intolerant of all spirit of advance or change, singularly devoid of tact, but literal, honest, and well-meaning. Moreover, he was absolutely self-satisfied, but utterly lacking in the sense of fun which makes conceited people so much less disagreeable, since it gives them a glimmering appreciation of their own absurdity.

As far as his outward man was concerned, the Reverend Gabriel Hornblower was not fair to look upon. Although Mrs. Pennypoker never failed to speak of him as "old Dr. Hornblower," in reality he was not far from forty-five; but he looked a score of years older, for his constant exposure to the fierce mountain gales and the burning suns of summer had tanned and dried him until his complexion closely resembled a withered seckel pear, and his body was as thin and wiry as that of a September locust in a season of famine. But, in spite of his dull, yellow-brown skin, his deep-set blue eyes retained all their old life and sparkle, while his thick auburn hair was cut close at the back and sides of his head, and allowed to grow long above his forehead, where it was combed up to form a single curl, which ran straight across the top of his head, from brow to crown. The peculiar nature of this curl had beguiled the time of dreary sermons for many a youthful sinner; for, like Melchisedek, it appeared to have its beginning and ending in nothing, and there was a certain fascination in tracing its placid course above the august forehead.

Approaching nearer to Dr. Hornblower, it was easy to see that he was a close student, either of books or of human nature. His habit of profound thought had developed an anxious frown, which had traced three deep wrinkles between his eyebrows; while, upon the rare occasions when his massive brain was at rest, and his brow was smoothed, two narrow lines of white, untanned skin came to the surface, and gave his face a little the appearance of a fantastic mask.

As he drew near the little group on the steps, Louise courteously rose to greet him.

"Come in, Dr. Hornblower," she said hospitably. "Walk into the parlor, and I'll call Mrs. Pennypoker."

The doctor paused irresolutely, while he looked up into her fair young face.

"Um--thank you," he said awkwardly. "I will--at least I didn't exactly come to see Mrs. Pennypoker, this afternoon. I"--

"Shall I call Wang Kum?" suggested Grant, with an air of ready interest, as he rose and moved a step towards the door.

"Not just now," said the Reverend Gabriel stiffly. "Miss Everett, may I not have the--the pleasure of sitting at your feet?" And he fixed his eyes on the patent-leather tips of her shoes.

"Of course we should be very glad to have you with us, Dr. Hornblower," returned Louise, while the pink color in her cheeks grew a shade deeper, as she heard an irrepressible giggle from Marjorie. "Ned, will you please bring out another chair? This is Charlie MacGregor, Dr. Hornblower," she added, as she saw the doctor's eyes turn inquiringly in his direction.

"In--deed; the young boy who was injured while at play? How do you do, Charles?" asked the Reverend Gabriel, after pausing to contemplate the lad, who had risen to his feet.

"Very much better, thank you," replied Charlie, while Howard gave him a stealthy poke with his foot.

"Ah? I am glad to hear it, for I have been much interested in your case. I hope you are properly thankful that there is now some slight possibility that your sight may be restored to you."

"Take this chair, Dr. Hornblower," interposed Louise hastily, while Charlie turned an appealing face towards his cousins. "It is a long time since you have been here; Mrs. Pennypoker was speaking of it only yesterday."

"Yes, I have been much occupied with the duties of my calling," returned the Reverend Gabriel, as he seated himself in the low chair, which brought his bony knees almost on a level with his chin. "My time has been engaged in visiting the erring members of my flock; and now, to-day, I find that I have an hour in which to call on you."

"I hope you don't look upon me as an erring member," Louise said, laughing lightly.

"Pardon me, my dear young friend, no; you are misapprehending me," answered the doctor, with a stiff-necked bow which sent Grant and Marjorie into the house to laugh unseen. "I only wished to state that"--

"Cousin Euphemia will be here in a minute, Lou," interrupted Ned, reappearing in the doorway. "She saw the doctor coming, and she sent me out to say she'd be right here; she wants to talk up something about Wang. Come on, Charlie, I want to show you something in the house."

"Really," exclaimed the discomfited doctor, as he looked beseechingly at Louise; "I had no wish to disturb your cousin, Miss Everett. I trust that she did not feel that she ought to see me, if it is inconvenient."

"Not at all; she'll be delighted to see you," answered his young hostess, with a grateful glance at her brother as he disappeared through the open door.

"There!" said Ned triumphantly, as the children settled themselves inside the parlor. "We'll stay câched in here, out of the way; and maybe there'll be some fun before long, if Cousin Euphemia and the doctor get after Wang. He's been to our church all the time lately, ever since our choir started up; and Cousin Euphemia doesn't like it. I just heard her telling Wang to go out to them as soon as he could get ready."

Ned's suspicions were well founded. A few moments later Wang Kum came shuffling around the corner of the house, with his hat cocked defiantly on the back of his head, and his hands buried in the pockets of his loose blue toga.

"How do you do, Wang Kum?" asked the doctor, benevolently eyeing the stray lamb before him.

"Heap well," returned Wang Kum calmly, as he kept his eyes fixed on the ground, to avoid Mrs. Pennypoker's warning glance.

"I was afraid you were ill," observed the doctor, with an approving smile for his own crafty manner of approaching the subject.

"Uh?" inquired Wang Kum.

"I thought perhaps you might be sick," repeated the doctor. "I hadn't seen you at church lately."

Wang shook his head contemptuously.

"Wang no get sick," he remarked.

"Then why haven't you been to church?" asked the doctor.

But Wang Kum only replied with a scarcely perceptible shrug.

"Wang, didn't you hear Dr. Hornblower speak to you?" asked Mrs. Pennypoker sharply.

Wang still stood gazing on the ground and nodding his head in a slow, thoughtful way which communicated a rhythmic undulation to his pigtail. At Mrs. Pennypoker's question, he glanced up.

"Wang no likee your church," he answered coolly. "Pisplykal church heap lot better; smell good, sound good." He paused, then added, with a cunning twinkle in his little dark eyes, "Make heap washee for washee-shop." And, turning on his heel, he marched off towards the kitchen, with the air of a man who had solved vast economic problems.

CHAPTER IX.

CAMPING ON THE BEAVERHEAD.

The August sun was shining down from a cloudless sky. He had risen betimes that morning; but he was not the first one up in Blue Creek, for the dim light of the dawn had found Ned and Grant Everett dressed and flying about the house, while, farther up the street, Marjorie was peering out through the window blinds, to assure herself that it was to be a pleasant day. By seven o'clock the Burnams, too, were stirring; and soon afterwards Allie and the boys appeared in the dining-room at the Everetts', to exchange noisy congratulations over the fine weather.

The day had at length come when they were to start upon their long-delayed camping trip. For the past week, the young people had been in a state of ferment, while their elders were in much the same condition, even to Mrs. Pennypoker, whose excitement was largely mixed with dread at the thought of the Bohemian life before her. The engineering camp, which they were to join, was now pitched beside the Beaverhead River; and Mr. Burnam, who had been out with his party much of the time since Charlie's accident, had come back to Blue Creek two days before, announcing that all was in readiness for their reception; so the hour for their departure was fixed upon. The distance to the camp was so great that they were to be two days upon their journey, spending the night at a ranch on their way, and reaching camp late on the following afternoon.

By nine o'clock, the party had assembled at the Burnams', ready for the start. They made an imposing cavalcade as they moved away down the street, for all but the older women were mounted on horseback. At the head of the procession rode Mr. Everett, Mr. Burnam, and Mr. Fisher, followed closely by the four boys, Allie and Marjorie, while Louise Everett, in her close-fitting dark green habit, cantered along in the rear, with Dr. Brownlee by her side. Then came the three wagons, the first driven by Wang Kum, with Janey perched up on the high seat beside him, eyeing her companion askance; while Mrs. Pennypoker, directly behind them, watched them both with an unswerving vigilance, ready to check any sign of levity on the part of man or maid. Mrs. Pennypoker was attired with all her wonted nicety, and her prim black straw bonnet and decorous gloves formed a striking contrast to the plain rough-and-ready gowns and broad hats of the other matrons, who were more accustomed to the needs of the life before them. Last of all came the two baggage wagons, one carrying the tents and stove, the other laden with the generous stock of provisions which Mr. Burnam had laid in for his guests; while in and out among them all raced Ben in a series of mad, elephantine gambols, expressive of his joy at being started for the field again.

Through the town they proceeded quietly enough; then, when they came out into the open ground of the lower cañon, the boys uttered a wild whoop, and dug their heels into the flanks of their ponies, as they went scurrying away, far in advance of the rest of the party.

"Just look at Charlie!" said Marjorie, as the boys turned to ride leisurely back to their companions once more. "He acts as if he didn't know what to do next."

"He's just about wild to be out again," returned Allie, gathering up her reins preparatory to joining the lads at the head of the procession. "You see, he was shut up 'most eight weeks, so I don't wonder he wants to make up for it. I expect he'll break his neck, though; for he's so near-sighted that he can't see without his glasses, and of course he can't wear them with that patch over his eye."

"How long is he going to wear it?" asked Marjorie soberly.

"I don't know; a good while, the doctor says, but I don't think Charlie minds much, after the other."

"I suppose he came awfully near"--Marjorie paused, with a little shiver.

Allie nodded understandingly.

"Yes; he didn't have any idea of it, though, till that day he met Dr. Hornblower at the Everetts'. After that he was dreadfully blue; you know he wouldn't stir out anywhere, for ever so long."

"Say, Allie," began Marjorie abruptly; "do you remember that day before he was hurt?"

"When you were so cross?" inquired Allie mercilessly.

"Yes. Did Charlie ever say anything about it?"

"Why, no," answered Allie after a little reflection. "I don't believe he ever thought of it again."

"I am glad of it," responded Marjorie; but still she did not look altogether pleased. She would have preferred that her words should carry a little more weight. Then she went on with her confession, "Well, I kept thinking about it, till I began to feel as if I'd done it all. You know I said I hoped something would happen. I wanted to come straight down here, that very night, but mamma wouldn't let me, not even long enough to just say I was sorry; and then the doctor wouldn't let any of us see him for ever so long, so I never said anything about it. Would you now, or would you let it go?"

"I don't know," said Allie thoughtfully. "Charlie'd never lay up anything of that kind; but I always just like to say I'm sorry, when I've been hateful to him or Howard. It kind of smoothes things out; but you can do as you like."

"Hi, you girls!" exclaimed Grant, dashing past them at this moment, after capering about the wagons in a manner calculated to bring down Mrs. Pennypoker's denunciations upon his yellow head. "What makes you so puppywented slow? Come on!"

"All right!" And Allie scampered off at his heels, sitting very straight and trim in her pretty new saddle.

Howard and Ned went after them, and Charlie was just ready to follow when he heard some one coming up behind him on his blindfold side.

"Wait just one minute, Charlie," said Marjorie's voice in his ear. "I want to say something to you--just to say"--She paused, and swallowed hard for a minute; then she went on steadily, "how sorry I've been that I was so mean to you that day your eye was hurt. I wanted to tell you so right off then, but I couldn't. But I kept thinking about it, all the time you were ill, and 'twas most as bad as if I'd thrown the ball." Marjorie stopped; the very earnestness of her apology made it hard to utter.

Charlie turned his head to look at her. He was surprised to see her face so pale and her lips trembling.

"That's all right enough, Marjorie," he said heartily. "I knew you didn't mean it, and I didn't think any more about it. Give us your fist, and then we'll go after the others."

Sunset, the next night, found the party comfortably established in their new quarters, on the very bank of the willow-bordered creek that plunged into the river, forty feet away. Across the creek and six hundred feet down the valley, dingy and brown with much service stood the tents of the engineering corps; but the officers' tent was deserted, for its occupants had come over to pay their respects at Camp Burnam, as the children had christened it. The site for the camp had been fixed upon, two days beforehand, and it was but the work of an hour to unpack the wagons and pitch the four tents which made up the outfit. At the south were the sleeping-tents, with Mrs. Burnam presiding over one, and Mr. Everett over the other, while at the east, close to the creek, were those given up to dining and cooking, where Janey and Wang Kum held sway by day, with many a wrangle over the possession of the little camp-stove, and many a heated discussion as to the relative merits of Asiatic and African cookery.

The stove had been the first thing to be unpacked, and by the time the last guy-rope was made fast, the last roll of bedding opened and arranged in its place, the welcome call to supper was sounded, and they gathered about the long table, spread in the open air, in the golden sunset light. Then the elders settled themselves for the evening, glad to rest after their long ride, while the children raced up and down the camp, exploring all the nooks and corners of their little domain, before throwing themselves down on a pile of blankets to watch the full moon as it rose from a bank of cloud just above the low hills to the eastward, and threw its white light over their gay group. Fifteen feet away from them Mrs. Burnam sat in the doorway of her tent, with Louise at her feet. The girl's golden hair was glistening in the moonlight, as she raised her head to speak to the topographer of the party, a sandy-haired, jovial young fellow, so lately come from "Sheff" that he retained all the slang and easy assurance of the genuine college boy. Ten months of camp life had made him hail with delight the prospect of paying court to a pretty girl; and he had attached himself to her side to the utter exclusion of Dr. Brownlee and the grave, taciturn leveller, who had retired from the contest and was devoting himself to Mrs. Burnam, whom he had known for years. For a few moments, the doctor stood looking on; then he turned away and joined the group of children, who received him enthusiastically.

"I'll tell you what, this is fine!" said Charlie contentedly, while the doctor seated himself by his side, and the boy stretched himself out at full length, with his head on his friend's knee, and lay staring up at the moon. "This is something I've never tried before, and always wanted to."

"Which?" inquired Allie, as she bent over to tickle his nose with a long straw stolen from the bedding; "taking up twice as much room as belongs to you, or looking at the moon?"

"Camping out, of course," answered her cousin, curling up his feet, in deference to her words. "Looking at the moon, too, for that matter; for I didn't see much of the last one."

"Speaking of moons," interposed Grant, from the corner where he and Marjorie and Howard had been chattering and giggling together; "the last two days have been no end hard on the storm center, and I think we shall catch a blizzard soon, by the looks. Just see her now!"

Grant's comment was in part justified, for the past two days had been undeniably hard upon Mrs. Pennypoker's appearance. The sun is no respecter of persons, and he had beaten down upon her majestic Greek nose with precisely the same fervent caresses which he had lavished upon Marjorie's freckled pug. Unfortunately, Mrs. Pennypoker's neat little straw bonnet was by no means so good a protection as Marjorie's soft scarlet felt hat, with its broad, flapping brim, and, even in the cold light of the moon, Mrs. Pennypoker's countenance gleamed with the luster of polished mahogany, which was enhanced by the great white kerchief that she had tied over her head, to keep out the evening air. No urging could induce her to sit on a blanket on the ground; so, in the absence of upholstered chairs, Mr. Everett had arranged a wooden pail against a tall box, cushioned them both with straw and blankets, and mounted his cousin upon this rustic throne, where she sat with her skirts carefully tucked up about her and her nose in the air, looking as much out of place as a Dresden china dinner service would have done on the rough board table.

Howard laughed, as he looked at her.

"I should think Wang would like her, to put her in his Joss house," he said disrespectfully. "What'll she ever do, before two weeks are up? She'll be a case for the doctor, sure enough."

"We ought to have brought Dr. Hornblower along, to amuse her," suggested Grant. "Come, I'm tired of this; let's have a game of 'I spy.' This moonlight would be fine for it. Come on, Ned!"

"Where?" inquired Ned lazily, for he was thoroughly absorbed in the story that Dr. Brownlee was telling.

"'I spy'; anything to get waked up."

"Sha'n't. I'm too comfortable to move."

"Allie?"

"Don't want to," replied Allie, without stirring from her place beside Ned.

"Charlie--anybody?" demanded Grant.

"What's the use? I can't see enough without my gigs."

"Lazy things! Don't disturb them, Grant," said Marjorie scornfully. "If this is the way you're going to do, I wish we'd left you at home. Grant, we'll hide, and let Howard find us. Come ahead!" And they vanished into the shadow beside the cooking tent.

Three minutes later there was a vigorous splash, followed by a shriek from Marjorie, which brought the whole party flying to the spot. Down in the shallow creek sat Grant, blinking up at them in bewilderment, as he wiped the water from his eyes.

"What's the matter?" asked Howard, as Mr. Burnam helped the boy to scramble to his feet, and up the steep bank of the stream.

"Wish you'd whitewash those guy-ropes!" responded Grant petulantly. "I tripped over 'em, and they landed me in that squdgy old creek. Marj needn't have squealed like a cat, though, and given it all away."

"'If this is the way you're going to do, I wish we'd left you at home,'" quoted Allie majestically, as she surveyed the dripping boy before her. "I think Charlie has his spectacles in his pocket, Grant, if you'd like to borrow them."

However, this ended the frolic of the evening, for Mrs. Pennypoker summarily seized upon the young explorer and ordered him to bed, while Wang Kum spread his clothes to dry before the fire. The other boys soon followed Grant's example, and the older people with them; so, after much wriggling and nestling about in the blankets, they at last dropped to sleep, and silence descended upon Camp Burnam.

Camp life began in earnest the next day, and for the next two weeks the party enjoyed one perpetual picnic. The children were up and out by daybreak, ready for the long days of fun, and by seven o'clock the breakfast call had sounded to gather them around the long table. It was good to see Wang Kum, tin horn in hand, emerge from his improvised kitchen, and blow the deep blast which should summon his flock to the meal; it was good to see Janey follow in his wake, armed with the great coffee-pot and a pile of light hoe-cakes, and then rush up and down behind the chairs, trying to serve them all at once, while she struggled in vain to repress an inclination to prance, and never failed to give a vigorous tweak to Wang Kum's pigtail, as she passed him. The relation between the two servants was unique, and, at times, somewhat strained. Although Wang Kum, left to himself, would have been the most peaceable of mortals, Janey persisted in treating him as an embodied joke, and lost no opportunity to tease and torment him, until he came to regard her with a strange mingling of hatred and fear.

"Wang tell Mis' Pen'plok'," he would mutter, with a threatening glance from his beady eyes.

"Ol' mis' won' believe you," Janey would make answer. "She knows dat you's a heathen, an' won' go to church. Cut off your great long plat, ef you don' wan' me to pull it no mo'. I cyarn' help it, ef it gits in my way, all de time." And then she would slyly lift the tip of the offending member and lay it across the table, before setting her heavy iron dish pan upon it. "Don' you year ol' mis' calling you?" she would ask then. "Take care! Don' upset all my dish tub!" And the war would begin again.

The weather left nothing to be desired, and, the party usually scattered soon after breakfast. The older men went on long hunting expeditions, in pursuit of the game which generally proved to be just over the divide; or explored the creek in search of trout,--great, rich-flavored fellows, which put to shame the tiny products of our Eastern streams. The boys, in the mean time, made friends with the engineers, and spent whole days in the field. Howard and Ned attached themselves to the transitman, and took turns as head and rear chain, while Grant superintended the levelling, and Charlie trudged along in the rear with the young topographer, who had taken a sudden fancy to the boy, and gave him frequent lectures on the theory and practice of surveying, until his pupil longed for the time when he too could wear on his watch-chain the tiny blue shield, with its golden date and initials.

Then there were long rides up and down the valley, and merry evenings in camp, when they told over the adventures of the day, played games, or sang college songs to the tinkling notes of the mandolin which Louise had brought with her. There was an elaborate afternoon tea, when Mrs. Burnam and Louise devoted their entire supply of tin plates and cups to the entertainment of the whole corps of engineers, down to the very axmen, and feasted them upon the miscellaneous delicacies concocted by Janey and Wang. Three days later, this hospitality was returned by a grand dinner-party at the lower camp, when venison and trout were the main dishes of the meal, and the table was set and served with a masculine disregard for appearances.

But the last night of their holiday had to come. Evening found them all gathered at Camp Burnam, watching the darkness settle around their pleasant forest home. Both camps were to be struck on the following day, for the engineering party was to move down the river at the same time that the others started for home.

"I have only two things to mourn about," said Charlie meditatively. "I haven't shot a single bear, and I haven't even seen the tail of a cayote."

"Wish you had; 't would have been such fun to see you turn and run," responded Ned, as he indolently settled himself with his head on Ben's side.

"Poor old Ben! Does he use you for a pillow?" asked Marjorie, stooping to stroke the great creature's head.

"I say, Marjorie, stop that," remonstrated Howard suddenly. "When you pet that end of him, this end wags, and his tail whacks awfully. Do let him go to sleep, or else warn me, so I can get out of the way."

"You'd better try this, you fellows," advised Ned. "It's fine; the best bed I've had since I left home."

"What's going on here?" asked Dr. Brownlee, moving up to the group, in company with Louise and her faithful attendant, the topographer, just as Howard and Charlie stretched themselves out beside Ned.

"Nothing, only they're getting ready for a nap," said Allie. "Don't you wish we didn't have to go home to-morrow?"

"I do," groaned Charlie. "I never had so much fun before, and I don't want to go back to town again. I believe I'll run off and set up in life as a brave. Will you come, too, Allie?".

"Not if I have to live in a wick-i-up three feet square, and wear your cast-off blankets," she answered, with some spirit. "I'm just about the right color for a squaw, though; that is, if I look as badly as the rest of you do."

"Thank you, dear," returned Howard laughing. "You're at least ten shades blacker than anybody else; and Charlie is so dark that his patch hasn't showed any for five days."

"How about the freckles?" inquired Charlie composedly. "I don't care; I've had a good time, and maybe 'twon't be fast color."

"It won't hurt you, Charlie," remarked the doctor. "You started off looking rather too white, after living in the dark for a month. This camping trip has been the best thing you could have had."

The two weeks had certainly done the boy good, and, removed from any temptation to use his eyes, he had given them the utter rest which they demanded, until they had nearly regained their former strength. Dr. Brownlee watched him approvingly for a moment. Notwithstanding the dark sunburn on his cheeks and the shade over his right eye, it was an attractive face, in spite of its lack of real beauty, such as had fallen to the share of Ned and Grant.

"It has been immense," said the boy regretfully. "But maybe we can come out again, next summer."

"Don't flatter yourself with any such notion," said Howard. "If you'd been with papa as long as I have, you'd know that there isn't much chance of our being here, by another summer. He may be ordered to Alaska or Arizona, by that time; and we'll have to 'hoppee 'long, too.'"

"Just this way," interposed Grant, starting up abruptly with an inviting chirrup to Ben, who scrambled to his feet with a suddenness which sent the three boys rolling into an indiscriminate pile among the blankets, as their pillow went rushing away across the camp, in pursuit of some imaginary intruder.

It was late that night when the party finally broke up and went to their tents; it was later still before the usual gentle snores arose from Mrs. Pennypoker's corner. Soon afterwards, the silence of the night was broken by the sound of stealthy footsteps, coming up the river bank from the engineers' tents. A moment later, the music from a full orchestra of combs roused the sleepers from their dreams.

"Farewell, farewell, my own true love!" they wailed, in a gusty and oft-repeated chorus, until even Ben's feelings overpowered him, and, running to the door of the tent, he raised his nose towards the waning moon, and howled till his voice was husky. Then the swaying curtain at the doorway of the tent dropped once more, and all was still. The play was over, and the orchestra had ceased. Camp Burnam's story was ended.

CHAPTER X.

UP THE GULCH.

"I do believe every-day things are pleasantest, after all," said Allie contentedly.

It was a month after their camping party, and she and her mother were comfortably settled in the parlor, with the mending basket between them. The windows and doors were thrown wide open, and the room was flooded with the yellow sunlight that lay across the floor, while the warm September wind softly fluttered the light draperies. Outside the door, on the piazza, Ben lay snoozing in the sun, sleepily wagging his tail in some happy dream of full-flavored bones or trespassing cats; and beyond him Victor was trudging up and down the path in front of the house, laden with a tiny scarlet pail filled with sand. Allie glanced thoughtfully about the pretty room, and out at her baby brother; then she turned back to her mother again, as Mrs. Burnam asked,--

"How do you mean, Allie?"

"Why, after all our camping and fun, it seems good to sit down and visit a little, mammy. Don't you see, we haven't had a chance for ever so long, not since Charlie was hurt; and I enjoy it, once in a while. The other is fun; but I like to stop and talk it over sometimes." And Allie paused meditatively, with one of Howard's long stockings drawn over her hand.

"Yes, I know," her mother answered, while she trimmed a patch to fit the hole which it was intended to fill; "we haven't had a quiet afternoon for a long time, hardly since Charlie came out here, last spring. You've been so busy with the boys that I didn't know whether you'd ever enjoy sitting down with me any more."

"Yes, this is nicest," said Allie. "The boys aren't you, any more than Charlie is Howard. I like them both; but I need you to straighten out things sometimes."

"What is it now?" asked her mother quietly, for she saw from Allie's face that something was troubling her, and, mother-like, she wished to help her little daughter.

"Why, it isn't so much; only something that Grant was telling, something Mrs. Pennypoker said," answered Allie, while she threaded her needle and stuck it in beside the hole. Then she asked abruptly, "Mamma, is it true that Charlie has ever so much money?"

"Yes; that is, he will have, when he grows up," replied Mrs. Burnam, a little surprised at the question, for she had tried to train her children to feel that wealth was by no means the main end in life.

"How much?" persisted Allie.

"A great deal, for Uncle Charlie was a rich man, and our Charlie is his only child."

"Oh!" And Allie lapsed into silence again.

"What made you ask, Allie?" her mother inquired, after a pause.

"Nothing; only Mrs. Pennypoker said somebody told her he was very rich, and that was the reason you'd let him come here, so maybe we could get some of it; and she asked Mrs. Pennypoker if she hadn't seen the way I hadn't had so much to do with Ned and Marjorie since he'd been here, and all. Wasn't it horrid, mamma?"

Mrs. Burnam frowned. She was sorry to have such ideas put into the head of her young daughter; and, during the past five months, she had grown to feel that Charlie was almost one of her own children; so the worldly-wise tone of these comments grated upon her ears.

"Grant had no right to tell you this," she said thoughtfully.

"I don't care if he did," Allie interrupted. "I knew 't wasn't true, and I told him that I didn't think Charlie had any money, and we didn't want any of it, if he had; we'd plenty of our own. But I wish people wouldn't talk such things. I like Ned and Marjorie just as well as I used to; but when Charlie's here in the house, and just as splendid as he can be, I don't see why I shouldn't like him better. Nobody minded when I was with Howard 'most all the time, and Charlie's just like another brother." And she nodded conclusively as she resumed her work.

Mrs. Burnam watched her steadily for a moment, trying to read whether there was any unspoken thought in her daughter's mind; but Allie looked up, and her blue eyes met her mother's so squarely that Mrs. Burnam was satisfied.

"Charlie does seem just like one of us," she assented heartily; "and I know we've all enjoyed his being out here; but it isn't because he's rich that we've liked him, it's because he's just what he is, a bright, manly boy, without any airs or nonsense. Aunt Helen asked to have him come to us, because he hadn't any other cousins; and it would have been a pleasant six months for all of us, if it hadn't been for his terrible illness." Mrs. Burnam paused; she could never speak of his accident without a shudder.

"I'm glad it happened," returned Allie proudly. "If it hadn't, we shouldn't ever have known how brave he was. And, besides, if it hadn't been for that, we never should have known Dr. Brownlee half so well, and he wouldn't have gone into camp with us; so you see there was some good came out of it. But didn't we have a fine time in camp, mammy?"

"Yes, I think our camping trip was a success, in more ways than one," said Mrs. Burnam, smiling quietly to herself, as she recalled certain scenes in which Louise and the doctor had played a part. There was no doubt in her mind about the enjoyment of two of their number, however the others might have looked upon it.

"But, after all," resumed Allie, going back to her original statement; "I do like getting settled down again; and this vacation has been so stirred up that I believe I shall be glad to have some lessons once more."

"Here comes Ned," said her mother, glancing up from her work as the boy turned the corner and came up the street towards the house. "He's probably after you and the boys for some frolic or other."

"All right; I've just finished my last stocking. Did you ever see anybody make such holes as Howard does?" And she rolled the stockings into a ball and tossed them into the basket, as Ned came up the steps.

"Hullo!" he remarked, dropping into the chair from which Allie had just risen, and helping himself to her orderly work-basket. "Where are the other fellows?"

"They've gone up the creek fishing," answered Allie, watching, with an anxious face, while Ned investigated her papers of needles, and then turned his attention to her button bag.

"They must want something to do," returned Ned scornfully. "I should think you about lived on fish, up here."

"They don't often catch anything," said Mrs. Burnam, laughing; "not even colds. Howard fell into the creek, day before yesterday, and then sat around in his wet clothes all the afternoon; but it didn't seem to hurt him any."

"I tried that once," said Ned, as he stealthily put the basket on the floor, just behind Allie, where she could not fail to step in it and overturn it; "but I had the worst of it, for Cousin Euphemia saw me when I came home. She put me to bed, right in the middle of the day, and made me take some hot ginger-tea. Ugh, what a mess 't was! I'd rather have had a dozen colds than be choked to death, and left to stew in a flannel blanket. But what I came to say, Allie--Oh, isn't that too bad! You've upset your basket."

"What a wretch you are, Ned!" And Allie slyly dropped a large, flat button down inside his collar, as she stooped to pick up her scattered treasures. "You've done this before, and I know just how sorry you are."

"I didn't do a single thing," returned Ned innocently. "How'd I know you were going to put your foot in it that way? But I stopped to see if some of you didn't want to go up the gulch this afternoon. It's not so very warm, and Lou and Grant are going, so I said I'd hurry on ahead and get you to come too. Here they are, now."

"I'll go; wait till I get my hat." And Allie vanished.

"Come along too, Mrs. Burnam," said Ned persuasively.

"I wish I could, Ned; but I must stay with Vic, for Janey has gone out this afternoon. You'd better stop in here, all of you, when you come back, though. The boys will be home by that time, and I want to see Louise, too," she added, as Ned and Allie went down the steps.

At the west side of the town, the mountains rose up, sheer and straight, their slopes ending abruptly at the outer streets, which were carefully laid out and numbered, although no houses had yet been built there. However, the low, even ground was elaborately divided into blocks, and the blocks, in their turn, into building lots, to be in readiness for the possible purchaser, who might appear at any moment. On the boundary line between the town and this suburban region was the little brick school-house; and beyond it lay the open ground which now, in the absence of any inhabitants, was still used as a wood yard for the distant smelter, whose constant fires easily devoured the vast piles of wood daily unloaded by the trains which ran down the spur of track leading to the yard. Beyond this again were the mountains, which rose to their highest point just to the west of the town, where the tips of the tallest peaks were always blanketed with the soft, white piles of snow. At only one spot their unbroken front was interrupted, where a deep, narrow ravine led far up among the mountains, forming a delightful walk in a warm summer day. After the burning glare on the dry, sandy soil of the town, which, in its barren lack of grass and trees, stared back at the sun like a lidless, lashless eye, the cool shadows of the pines in the gulch were a refreshing change. The little gulch had its variety of names: Bear Gulch, it was called, Lover's Gulch, and even Cemetery Gulch, from the lonely burial ground perched on the top of the rugged bluff at its entrance.

Ned and Allie had taken the lead, with Louise and Grant following close behind them, as they picked their way among the countless tin cans scattered over the fields, or paused to look and laugh while the boys clambered to the top of the long wood-piles, and ran slow, unsteady races over their uneven surfaces. Then they came out to the track, and followed along its course, where Ned and Allie joined hands and walked the rails, and Grant trudged along behind them, stepping with an elaborate care upon each one of the ties, or leaping over occasional cattle-guards, as they crossed his path.

They were far past the western houses of the town, and rapidly approaching the foot of the mountain, when Ned gave Allie's hand a violent twitch.

"Look back!" he exclaimed in an undertone.

With a little cry of alarm, Allie sprang from the track; then, as she glanced back over her shoulder, she burst out laughing.

"How you scared me, Ned!" she said, as she stopped abruptly. "I thought 'twas a train, but it's only Dr. Hornblower."

True enough; up the track behind them came the excellent doctor, waving his cane in amicable salutation, as he strode along at a pace which might have put to shame the wearer of the famous seven-league boots. His leathery skin was dark and shining from the violence of his exercise, as he came sweeping on towards them, till he paused by the side of Louise, who watched him with some anxiety while he stood wheezing and panting before her.

"My dear Miss Everett," he said, when he could regain his breath enough to speak once more; "are you not afraid to walk so rapidly at this altitude? I fear you may over-exert yourself some day." He paused for a moment, puffing like the engine of an overloaded freight train; then he resumed, "I called at your residence, and was so regretful at not finding you at home that your cousin, Mrs. Pennypoker, told me that you were bound for the gulch, and assured me that there was--um--some prospect of my overtaking, not to say catching up with you."

"Are you out on the round-up again to-day, Dr. Hornblower?" asked Ned soberly.

The Reverend Gabriel looked at him with a perplexed countenance.

"I am afraid that I do not perfectly apprehend your meaning," he said.

"Why, you said, last time you called on Lou, that you were hunting up stray sheep, and I didn't know but you were out after some more to-day," Ned explained, with a naughty satisfaction in his sister's struggles to repress her smiles.

But Dr. Hornblower was quite unmoved. His professional dignity rose to the surface, and his voice took on its Sunday twang as he replied pompously,--

"No, Edward; the sheep are all in the fold. To-day I am only in search of congenial society." And he bowed gravely to Louise.

"Come on, now," whispered Grant, as he joined Allie and Ned in advance, and left Louise to follow them with her elderly admirer; "the doctor's lost his wind already, and can't keep up; but, if he wants a walk, we'll give him one."

His companions entered into the spirit of his proposition, and they quickened their pace, after casting one backward glance towards Louise, as she lingered along, with a sort of repressed impatience of step and manner, while she listened to the Reverend Gabriel's elaborate explanations of his reasons for following her. Then such a race as they led him! Quitting the track, they turned aside into the open ground, covered with uneven tufts of coarse bunch grass and thickets of sage brush, now racing down a little hillock, now jumping over a tiny stream and forcing their way through the clumps of willows on the bank, but always choosing the roughest, hardest path, and always going at the top of their speed, while Louise and the doctor panted and floundered along too far in the rear to be heard in their calls for mercy. Even Allie was beginning to be exhausted when, a few hundred feet above the mouth of the gulch, Grant turned abruptly to the right and scrambled up the steep hillside leading to the cemetery.

"There!" he chuckled, while Ned and Allie, breathless with laughing and with their rapid climb, dropped down on the ground beside him; "we'll give him a rest when he gets up here. If he's going to come along and spoil all our fun, he must pay for it; but he'll be tired by this time."

"I wonder if he'll ever get up here alive," said Allie, as she reached out to the nearest bush, to pick a bit of fur from the twig which had caught it from some passing cottontail. "You almost used me up, and I don't believe Miss Lou could have gone on much farther, so I shouldn't wonder if he was pretty nearly dead."

"Well, 'twould be a nice, convenient place for the funeral; only I shouldn't be surprised if he stuck, half way up here," suggested Ned, comfortably lying on his back, and fanning himself with the hat which Allie had tossed aside. "No; here he comes," he added, as the Reverend Gabriel's wide-brimmed straw hat and flushed face appeared over the brow of the hill, followed by Louise, looking rosy and mischievous, but as fresh as she had done at the start.

"Come over to this tree, doctor, and sit down here in the shade while you rest," she said kindly, as she led the way to the spot where the boys were stretched out on the grass.

There was an unwonted gentleness in her voice, for she had been quick to discover the impish intention of her brothers, and was anxious to atone for their lack of courtesy towards an acquaintance whom she had always regarded as an old man, on the down-hill side of life. In spite of herself she had been amused at the doctor's frantic efforts to keep up with her own firm, quick pace, and at his urgent entreaties that she should tell him if he walked too fast for her. Nevertheless, as she seated herself beside her young brothers, she was resolving to give them a lecture upon the sins of the afternoon, so soon as she could get them in a place of safety.

In the mean time, the doctor appeared to be strangely annoyed over something, although she was unable to discover the cause of his trouble. In obedience to her inviting gesture, he had spread out his large blue silk handkerchief on the ground by her side, and seated himself upon it. Then he started to remove his hat; but he had no sooner raised it a little from his head than he hastily clapped it on again, with a little exclamation of surprise and displeasure.

"I do hope that these bad boys haven't given you too hard a climb, doctor," Louise was saying politely, while she turned to frown down any fresh demonstrations on the part of Grant, who was evidently plotting some new mischief.

"Um--m--ah--no--at least, I beg your pardon, but what was it you said?" inquired the doctor, so abstractedly that Louise looked at him in astonishment.

The Reverend Gabriel sat with his face slightly turned away from her. He was tilting his hat so that, on the farther side, it was raised an inch or two from his head, while, with his disengaged hand, he was feeling carefully about underneath it, as if in search of some missing object. His face, meanwhile, was rapidly assuming every appearance of trouble and distress, which became more and more acute with every fresh motion of his hand. Louise watched him compassionately, sure that something was amiss, but not daring to offer to come to his assistance; then, thinking to spare him any added mortification, she looked away towards the valley.

A lovely picture lay at her feet, for the cañon opened out before her eyes in all the grandeur of its mountainous surroundings, while the little town in its bosom was softened and beautified by the kindly autumnal haze, which took away the crude shabbiness of its detail and brought it into harmony with the rugged landscape about it. Beyond the town lay the creek, and over it all floated the heavy pall of thick white smoke, which seemed to be supported on the tall red chimneys of the smelter buildings. The sun was dropping behind the mountains, and already the town lay in shadow, while the last beams lingered upon the cloud of smoke which flushed to a pale pink, then deepened to a rosy glow. The girl's eyes rested on the scene below her; then, surprised at the continued silence of her escort, she glanced at him once more. He was still groping about underneath his hat, with the same strained, upward roll to his eyes; but, as she looked at him, a new light burst in upon Louise's mind, for two long locks of tawny hair had straggled down over his right ear, and lay in a feeble ringlet against the top of his tall collar. The Reverend Gabriel's wrist brushed against them; he felt of them inquiringly; then he deliberately took off his hat to show the top of his head shorn of the glory of his curl, and the long ends of hair hanging in elf-locks about his face.

"Miss--um--Miss Everett," he began hesitatingly, while a dark flush rose on his weather-beaten cheeks; "Miss Everett, I am exceedingly sorry to trouble you, but"--he paused; then went on desperately; "in fact, could you be good enough to lend me a hairpin? The exertion of my climb has removed mine from its accustomed place, and I fear that my hair may be slightly disarranged."

The silence that followed was unbroken while Louise felt about among her braids and drew out a long, slender pin; but when the doctor put his hat down on the ground by his side, carefully rolled up his hair over his two forefingers, spread it into the usual long curl, and fastened it into its place, Allie and Ned fell into an uncontrollable fit of giggling. But, for the once, Grant's attention was distracted, for he was gazing steadily towards the engine house at the mouth of the mine.

"Say, Lou," he exclaimed; "what's going on down there? Everybody's rushing over to the mine; something must be wrong."

Louise's eyes followed the direction of his hand.

"There 's some trouble, down there," she said, rising abruptly. "Will you excuse us, Dr. Hornblower, if we go down without waiting to get rested? I am always a little anxious about my father." And she hurried away down the hill, leaving the Reverend Gabriel to adjust his hairpin at his ease, while he reflected upon the unsatisfactory nature of his walk.

CHAPTER XI.

"SWEET CHARITY'S SAKE."

"You see," Howard was explaining to Ned, that evening, "he'd put in his charge for the blast, and was tamping it down all right; but he kicked over his drill, and the end fell on an extra package of giant powder."

"I know that," interrupted Ned. "Papa said he was outrageously careless, to have any of the stuff lying around loose; and 'twas a wonder that there weren't any more men near enough to be killed. Poor old Mike! He's worked in the mine ever since 'twas first opened, and he was one of their best men."

"I don't see how he came to be so careless, then," said Marjorie, wisely shaking her head over the matter. "I should suppose he'd have known better by this time."

"They do know better," said Ned thoughtfully; "only they get hardened to the risk and don't think much about it, or else say their luck will hold out. But Mike has the worst of it. Do you know, this is the first accident in the Blue Creek I ever remember, and I used to see Mike 'most every day, so I can't get to believe it a bit. It seems as if it couldn't be true."

"Papa was all broken up to-night," added Grant. "He knows all the old foremen, and Mike was the best one of them all."

"I believe I'd rather die 'most any way than be blown up," said Allie, with a shudder. "It must be so hard for his family. But didn't you say somebody else was hurt, Howard?"

"Just one boy," answered Howard, rising and walking nervously about the room, as the scene came freshly to his mind. "I don't know who he was, for nobody seemed to be sure of his name. He had dark hair, and was about Charlie Mac's size, I should think. They brought him up in the cage just as Charlie and I stopped at the shaft, and the first thing we knew, we were right beside him."

"What's it going to do to him?" asked Marjorie, as her bright face grew very serious at the picture that Howard had brought before her.

"No one knew, for the doctor wasn't there, of course, and they took him right off home. Papa said he was an English boy that lived over the creek," said

Grant, stretching himself out on the sofa, with his heels on the cushion.

Marjorie sprang up and shook herself, with a little shiver.

"Don't let's talk about it any more," she exclaimed. "It just makes me sick to think of it."

"But it's there, all the same, whether we talk about it or not; and if you'd seen it, as we did, you couldn't forget it, even if you did keep still," said Howard soberly; and Allie added,--

"Besides, maybe if we talk about it we can find out there's something to do, to help out."

For an hour, the five young people, gathered in the Everetts' parlor, had been telling over the details of the accident. As Ned had said, it had been a long time since the Blue Creek had been visited by an accident like those which so frequently occurred in the neighboring mines, and this, killing, as it did, one of the oldest and best-known of the miners, had created an intense excitement in the little town. Immediately following the explosion, there had been put in circulation a report of the accident so exaggerated that it had brought to the spot the wives of half the miners in the camp, each one of whom was confident that her husband was among the twenty or more men said to have been killed. It had been this hasty gathering which had caught Grant's eye; and the Everetts and Allie had hurried down into the town just in time to learn the truth that but one man was killed, and to watch the excited groups as they slowly dispersed, so noisy in their joy that their own friends had escaped, that they forgot to give more than a passing thought to poor, careless Mike, whose working days were ended. But that came later; and among all his mourners there were none more sincere than the little group at the Everetts', who knew and appreciated the real worth of the jovial, brawny Irishman, whose pleasant word and helping hand were extended to all with whom he ever came in contact. They were still talking of him when the bell rang; and, a moment later, Wang Kum ushered Dr. Brownlee into the parlor. At sight of him, Marjorie sprang up impulsively.

"Oh, doctor, tell us about the poor boy! How is he?" she asked abruptly, without waiting for any formal greeting.

"If you mean the one who was hurt at the mine this afternoon," the doctor was beginning, when Ned hastily interposed,--

"Hold on a minute, Dr. Brownlee; but don't sit down in that chair. There's something wrong about the stuff it's covered with; 'tisn't real leather, and it melts and gets sticky in summer, or when there's a hot fire. You'd better steer clear of it. We mean to keep it out of the way."

"You might use it for a trap," suggested the doctor laughingly, as he pushed aside the great easy-chair, and settled himself in a willow rocker. Then his face grew grave again, as he turned back to Marjorie. "He's as badly hurt as he can be," he went on. "He'll get over it, but he'll never be able to do anything more. He hasn't come to his senses yet, and I wish he needn't, for the present, for he has a hard time before him," he added, as he rose to meet Louise, who came into the room just then.

"I'm a little upset to-night," he said apologetically, in answer to her exclamation about the coldness of his hand. "To be perfectly honest, this is my first accident case; and it's a very different thing from seeing people quietly ill in bed, even if you know they can't get well. I was at the house when they brought him in, and I hope I sha'n't often have to go through such a scene again."

"Tell me about it," said Louise, with a gentle sympathy which lent a new grace to her beauty. "I'm not afraid to hear, and perhaps I can do something for them by and by."

And the doctor told, forgetting himself, and even the charming young woman before him, as he went on with the story of the mother's frantic sorrow over her only son, of the boy's half-conscious suffering, and of the long, helpless life before him. The girl's eyes filled with tears as she listened, though her pity for the lad was mingled with a new admiration for the speaker. The tale did not lie entirely in the mere words describing the accident; but, under all that, it told of the generous, kindly sympathy of the true doctor, who shrinks from the sight of pain, even while he gives his life to watching and helping it.

Two weeks later Marjorie was spending a stormy afternoon at the Burnams', when Ned appeared on the piazza.

"Hullo!" he exclaimed, as he furled his dripping umbrella, and shook himself out of his rubber coat. "You'd better believe I'm wet. Lou went off before it rained, and I had to pack her rubbers and umbrella over to her. It's no joke to walk a mile in such a pour."

"Where is she?" asked Allie, while she hospitably drew up a chair for her guest.

"Over the creek with that boy of hers. She puts in ever so much time there, since he's better. She says he's crazy to read and be read to, so she goes over 'most every day," responded Ned, as he wriggled away from the too exuberant caresses of Ben.

"How is he getting on?" inquired Marjorie.

"All right, as much as he can. Lou says he's bright and knows a good deal."

"How kind she's been to him!" said Allie thoughtfully. "And Charlie, too. He buys lots of things for him, and sends them over by Dr. Brownlee."

"Good for Charlie Mac! That's just like him," said Ned enthusiastically. "Where is he, anyhow?"

"We supposed he was over at your house with Grant," answered Howard from the corner where he sat, industriously whittling at a set of small wooden pegs.

"It must be nice to have money, and do all sorts of things like that," sighed Marjorie. "I can't afford to buy books and fruit, for I'm always short on my allowance; and mamma won't let me give up my lessons, even for one day, so I can't do what Miss Lou does."

"Poor Marj! It's a hard case; for time's money, and you haven't any of either," remarked Howard.

"Wait a minute!" she answered, starting from her chair, and pacing up and down the room, as was her habit when much absorbed. "I'm getting hold of an idea."

"Hold on, then, and don't let it go," advised Ned, dodging the sofa pillow that Marjorie hurled at him.

"Listen!" she commanded imperatively. "It's really and truly a good plan. You know we haven't any too much money, for we all of us spend our allowances faster than we get them; but let's begin to save, and put it all together, till by and by we can send him something."

"Good, Marjorie! What a splendid idea!" exclaimed Allie, fired with zeal at the thought.

"But, I say," remonstrated Howard; "how long are you going to keep up the scheme? I can save like a house afire, for a little while; but Christmas is coming, and I've promised to give Allie a rubber doll, and charity begins at home, you know. I'm willing to help on your lad for a month or so; but let's put a limit to it."

"I didn't think you'd be so stingy, Howard," said Marjorie, turning on him a gaze of virtuous sorrow.

"'T isn't stingy," retorted Howard; "it's common sense. I 'm as sorry for him as you are; but I think we'd better go easy on it a little, and see how we come out."

"Let's try it for a month," interposed Allie hastily, for she saw that Marjorie was growing indignant. "If we save all we can, we shall have a good deal by that time. What shall we get him?"

"A whole set of Henty's books," suggested Ned promptly.

"No; I think he'd like a tool-chest better," said Howard, eyeing with disfavor the shabby knife in his hand.

"What an idea, Howard! He couldn't use a tool-chest, even if he had one," said Allie, laughing disrespectfully at her brother's suggestion. "We want to get him something he could have the good of all the time. What do you say, Marjorie?"

"Miss Lou said he used to sing a good deal," observed Marjorie, her virtue coming to the surface once more. "Why wouldn't it be nice to get him one of the new hymnals; a great big one, with all the tunes in it? I think he'd find it very comforting."

A pause followed her words; then the boys burst into a shout of laughter. Marjorie looked a little aggrieved.

"I don't see what you're laughing at," she said, with a suspicion of a pout. "Hymns are a great deal better for such people than your crazy old books and tool-chests."

"Don't be a jay, Marjorie," said Ned bluntly. "He isn't any more *such people* than we are; and because a fellow is down on his luck he doesn't want everybody shying coffins at him. But here comes Grant; let's see what he says. Then we can save up for a month, and see how much we get; after that, we can tell better what to do with it."

For the next four weeks a spirit of miserliness seemed to have broken out among the young people, who scrimped and saved and denied themselves for days, only to succumb to the temptations of "just one little bit of a treat," which swept away most of their savings again, and left them no better off than before. The day after they had taken their great resolution, they went down town in a body, and invested most of the funds at the disposal of the syndicate in an elaborate toy bank, in the form of a dog who stolidly swallowed their stray bits of silver and nickel into an iron strong-box below, which nothing but a powerful hammer could ever succeed in opening. As soon as this purchase was made, and a nest-egg solemnly deposited in its miniature vault, their zeal cooled, and the dog was left in Allie's keeping for a week of slow starvation. It is true that Charlie often begged to be allowed to contribute from his own more abundant resources; but it had been agreed that he could only add one fifth to the combined offerings of the others; so, though the end of the month was fast approaching, the bank was still nearly as light as when it came from the store, and only responded with a faint rattle to Allie's frequent shakings.

Matters were in this condition, one day, when Grant dropped in for one of his frequent short calls on Marjorie.

"Mustn't stay," he answered briefly; "I'm on my way down to get my hair cut. I'm going to try Charlie Mac's barber; he gets a better shape on your hair, somehow."

"Extravagant boy!" said Marjorie reproachfully. "You'll have to pay him ever so much. How much does he charge, anyway?"

"Six bits," answered Grant, as he picked up his hat, and took hold of the door knob.

"That's perfectly shameful," said Marjorie. "It's ever so much more than you generally pay. I'll tell you what: I'll do it for you for ten cents, and you can have all the rest to put in our bank. You haven't begun to give your share."

"I can't help it; a fellow can't live on nothing," said Grant defensively. "I've only had two sodas and a new bat this week. Besides, I want my hair cut like Charlie's."

"I should think you would be ashamed to spend so much on just your looks, when you think of that poor, exploded boy," said Marjorie in a sanctimonious tone. "And then," she added persuasively, "if you let me cut it for ten cents, you can spend some for a treat and put the rest in the bank."

Grant wavered. The prospect of having an unexpected treat, and at the same time of putting a little money into their hoard was an attractive one; but, after all, his boyish soul was filled with a vain desire to see how his yellow hair would look, after being cut by Charlie's man. Moreover, Charlie's barber was an expensive luxury, and Grant had experienced some difficulty in coaxing the necessary funds out of Mrs. Pennypoker, so he had a little natural misgiving as to her opinion of his putting the money to other uses.

"You could get a soda, and ever so many pine nuts," went on the tempter, touching her victim's weakest spot.

Grant yielded a little.

"Have you ever cut anybody's hair?" he demanded.

"No; but I can, well enough. It's just as easy." And Marjorie gave her hand an impressive sweep through the air. "I know just exactly how," she added.

"You're sure you can make it look all right?" asked Grant again, while there floated through his mind a blissful vision of himself, tranquilly eating pine nuts, and of the others, standing grouped about him, praising his generosity.

"Course I can; why not?" said Marjorie scornfully. "Don't you s'pose I know how a boy's hair ought to look?"

"And you'll do it for ten cents?"

"Yes."

"All right; sail in!" And Grant dropped into a chair and closed his eyes, as if he were about to be decapitated.

"You needn't think I'm going to do it here in the parlor," said Marjorie. "It's going to make an awful muss; you must come out of doors."

"You needn't think I'm going to freeze," retorted the victim, opening his eyes to glare at her belligerently. "If I give you the job, and pay you all that for it, I'm going to have something to say about the way it's done. You can spread down a paper, if you're afraid."

"Well," said Marjorie reluctantly; "I don't know but 'twould be cold on the piazza. Wait a minute, and I'll be ready."

Her preparations were quickly made. A layer of newspapers was spread over the carpet, and a chair set out in the middle of the room. Then she tied a blue checked apron around Grant's neck, and announced herself as in readiness.

"Sit down there," she commanded, as she dived into a box of scrap-book materials for a pair of paste-stained scissors; "and don't you dare to wiggle, for I shall cut you if you do." And she gave the scissors an expressive clash above his head.

"All right," said Grant again, as he once more closed his eyes and assumed a look of abject misery.

Then silence fell upon the room, and for a long half hour the stillness was only broken by the clatter of the loose-jointed scissors, and an occasional moan from Grant, when the blunt points collided with his skin with more than ordinary vigor. With one hand clutching the boy's yellow head for support, Marjorie stood over him, clipping and trimming, then stopping to contemplate the result of her labors, before attacking a new spot. She had started out upon her undertaking valiantly enough; but a dozen reckless slashes had begun to awaken some slight misgivings in her mind, and she proceeded more slowly and with frequent pauses, while an anxious pucker about her brows showed that she was not entirely satisfied with her work. Worst of all, Grant was beginning to grow restive.

"'Most through?" he had inquired some time before.

But Marjorie had consoled him with assurances of his speedy release; and he had resigned himself to the inevitable and sat quiet for ten minutes longer. Then he burst out again.

"Say, Marjorie," he protested; "you scratch like fun; and you've been long enough about it to cut a dozen hairs. Hurry up, there!"

"I'm almost through," she answered hastily. "Your hair's so tough it takes me longer than I thought 'twould."

"How's it going to look?"

"Lovely!" responded Marjorie, with a fervor which she was far from feeling, while she made a few hurried clips at a long lock which, in some way, had escaped her vigilance. "There!" she added. "That's all. You can get up."

Grant rose and shook himself; then, with the apron still hanging about his neck, he marched to the nearest mirror and gazed at the reflection of his shorn head. It was a strange picture that met his eyes. His head was encircled with narrow furrows, where the scissors had done their work so well that not a spear of hair rose above the bare skin. These ridges were intermingled with patches of stubble of varying length; while, here and there, a long lock had escaped entirely, and, in the lack of its former support, now stood out from his scalp at an aggressive angle, like the fur on the back of an angry cat. The whole effect resembled nothing so much as a piece of half-cleared woodland, where the workman's axe had here levelled everything to the ground, here left a clump or two of bushes, and here spared an occasional giant tree which towered far above its fallen comrades, in the conscious pride of its unimpaired strength.

The result was novel; but Grant appeared to fail to appreciate it, for when he turned back to face Marjorie again his brown eyes were blazing, and he was well-nigh speechless with indignation.

"You beastly fraud!" he shouted, while he rubbed his hand over his denuded pate, with a tenderly caressing motion, as if to console it for its appearance.

"What's the matter?" asked Marjorie faintly.

"Matter!" stormed Grant. "Look at my head and see for yourself. You said you could cut my hair all right, and you've just spoiled it all. I won't pay you one cent. It'll take weeks and weeks for it to get back again."

"It looks all right," said Marjorie stubbornly; "and you've got to pay me. You said you would, and you never lie. The time I spent on it is worth more than ten cents, anyway."

"I sha'n't pay you," retorted Grant doggedly.

"You shall!"

"I won't!"

"Then I'll tell Allie and Charlie, and all the rest, that you're stingy and a great big cheat."

"Tell away if you're mean enough."

"And I'll tell Mrs. Pennypoker; and she'll send you to bed without your supper, for stealing her money."

"Didn't steal it!"

"Yes, you did, too! She gave it to you for something, and you were going to spend part of it for soda; that's stealing."

"'T isn't, either!"

"'T is, too, and you know it! And if you aren't ashamed of it why don't you want me to tell her?"

Grant saw that his enemy had outflanked him, and that his only possible course was to make the best terms he could.

"Now, see here," he said more quietly, as he pointed to his head again; "this isn't worth anything; but you've cornered me, so I can't get out. But, if I pay you, you must give me back a nickel, to pay for the hole you snicked out of my ear."

Marjorie's face fell. She had been hoping that he would not notice the little red spot on the tip of his left ear.

"And then," continued Grant remorselessly; "you can just put on your hat, and come along with me to Allie's. We'll each put a nickel in the bank, and then we'll be square. But you'd better believe I'll tell the boys who did this, so they won't get taken in as I did."

A week later, Charlie and Allie opened the bank and counted the funds. Only sixty-five cents had accumulated there; Allie's face fell as she surveyed the meagre hoard.

"Hush up!" commanded Charlie, as he dropped something yellow and shining into her lap. "I was in a bad fix last summer, and I know how 'tis, so I ought to help on more than the rest of you. You just keep still and don't say anything to the others."

And no one else ever knew the full history of the magazine that put in its appearance at the beginning of the following month, with a greeting to the stranger boy from his friends across the creek.

CHAPTER XII.

HOME WITHOUT A MOTHER.

There was mutiny in the Burnam household. It had broken out the night before, when Vic was saying his prayers in the presence of Mrs. Pennypoker, who was supposed to be temporarily filling his mother's place. At the petition for daily bread, Vic had stopped short.

"Go on," said Mrs. Pennypoker, in slow, measured tones.

Victor opened his eyes and glared at her with undevout opposition.

"Don't want bread," he said firmly. "Vic likes biskies."

"It means the same thing, Victor," answered Mrs. Pennypoker, in her hard voice. "Now be a good little boy and finish your prayer, or God won't listen to you, another time, when you are asking him for something."

It was then that Vic had delivered himself of his first baby heresy, which had been slowly working in his brain while Mrs. Pennypoker had been urging him through his devotions, in a manner so unlike the tender gentleness of his pretty mamma.

"I don't like your God," he said deliberately, as he gazed up into the cold, dark eyes above him; "I don't like your God a bit; I'm tired of him. I want my mamma's." And, rising from his knees, he dived into bed, where he burst out sobbing for mamma; nor would he be quieted until Mrs. Pennypoker had left the room, and sent Allie up to comfort her baby brother with repeated assurances that mamma would come by and by.

Two days before this, Mrs. Burnam had received a note from her husband, saying that a fall from his horse had bruised and strained him a little, and that it seemed best for him to stay a few days at a small country hotel, not far from his camp. In reality, it was only a slight affair; but Mrs. Burnam had felt so uneasy that she had resolved to go to him, to be at hand in case he might need any of the little attentions which it would be hard for him to get, in the small town where he was left. Since Victor would be only an additional care, she had decided not to take him with her; but, remembering the emergency which had arisen during her last absence, she had begged Mrs. Pennypoker to take charge of the household for the time that she was away from home.

This arrangement had not met with the entire approval of the young people, it must be confessed; for Howard and Allie had hoped to be allowed to pose as heads of the house, while Victor had lifted up his voice in vigorous protest against the intruder. However, until Victor's rebellion, the second night, there had been no open outbreak, although there was an undercurrent of antagonism between Mrs. Pennypoker and the children, which threatened an explosion at any moment. It was a new experience for Howard and Allie to have their fun and laughter repressed, and they were far from being ready to submit to it with a good grace; while Janey had promptly ranged herself upon their side, and manifested a monkey-like ingenuity in planning the pranks which were making Mrs. Pennypoker's frown grow deeper at every moment.

"Just look at Janey!" Howard had whispered to his sister, as the maid came in at dinner-time, with the strings of her dainty white cap tied under her chin, and the point standing up from her forehead like an old woman's poke bonnet.

Mrs. Pennypoker caught the whisper. Putting on her glasses, she turned to glare at Janey, who received her stare with an unmoved countenance.

"Jane," she said, with crushing dignity; "go back to the kitchen, and arrange your cap properly."

And Janey went, but it was not until she had given the two boys a look which upset their gravity and forced them to retire behind their napkins. She was gone for some moments, and when she reappeared her cap was drawn far down over her face, and she came tiptoeing in with short, mincing steps, to go through her serving with an exaggerated elegance, bowing and smirking and flourishing her tray, with all the airs and graces at her command. However, there was nothing to be done about it, and Mrs. Pennypoker was forced to be content with ignoring her for the present, while she frowned down any demonstrations of amusement on the part of the children. The rest of the meal was hurried through in silence, and as soon as it was over the young people shut themselves up in Allie's room, to vent their indignation by talking over the events of the past two days.

"You don't catch anybody getting in ahead of Janey, though," said Howard with a chuckle. "She's a match for even Mrs. Pennypoker."

"I'm 'most afraid she'll get mad and go off," said Allie anxiously. "Mrs. Pennypoker has just been nagging at her all day long, and Janey won't put up with it. She isn't used to it, as Wang Kum is."

"Even Wang Kum kicked, the other day," said Charlie, sitting down on the footboard of the bed, and swinging his heels while he talked. "Grant told me about it. Wang made a mistake and threw away all her soup she'd made, just before dinner; and when she scolded him for it, he said he ''ought 'twas dish-water.' She gave him fits, scolded like everything, till all at once he drew himself up and said: 'Old lady scold heap much; Wang no be bossed by hens.' And he turned and walked off, and left her standing there, with her mouth wide open."

"Good enough for her!" applauded Howard. "I only hope Janey'll serve her the same way."

"I don't believe I do," said Allie thoughtfully. "She's here, and we'll have to make the best of her. But don't you pity Ned and Grant, to have to stand her all the time?"

The predicted explosion was not slow in coming. Charlie had come in after his lessons, the next morning, clasping a huge watermelon in his arms, and, without a word to Mrs. Pennypoker, he had carried it through to the kitchen.

"Here, Janey," he called; "I'm awfully hungry, and if you'll cut this up for us to eat now, before lunch, I'll give you a quarter of it. You'd better do it, for it's the last one you'll get this year."

With the zeal of her melon-loving race, Janey's eyes glistened, as she received the treasure.

"Dat's a gay one, Mars' Charlie!" she exclaimed, as she snapped her fingers against its green rind, and listened delightedly to the clear, crisp sound. "Janey'll cut it right up for you, befo' she sets de table or anything. You all likes melons so well, you ought to see 'em we has down Souf. Reckon you'd jus' about bu'st you'selves, eatin' 'em."

She gave the melon one more ecstatic embrace, and dandled it fondly in her arms for a moment; then she laid it carefully down on the table, while she went for a knife.

"'Wa-a-atermelon! Green rind, red meat; All juicy, so sweet. Dem dat has money mus' come up an' buy; And dem dat hasn't mus' stan' back an' cry Wa-a-a-atermelon!'"

She crooned to herself, as she returned with the knife in her hand, and stuck it in, clear to the heart of the fruit before her.

"What's that, Janey?" asked Allie, who had followed Charlie out into the kitchen.

"Dat? Dat's a song I done heard an ol' man singin', one day. He had some melons to sell, out on de corner by my mudder's house, an' he kep' a singin' it ober an' ober. Ah, dat's a fine one!" she added contentedly, as the rich red heart of the melon appeared. She paused for a moment, then she cocked her head on one side, as she gazed rapturously at the great piece which Charlie offered her. "You all know how me an' my brudder use' to eat our melons, when mammy wan' roun' to smack us?" she inquired suddenly.

"How'd you do it?" asked Charlie, laughing.

"Dis way. See?" And clutching the piece in both hands, she buried her face in it, and began to devour it, much as a squirrel gnaws the meat out of a walnut.

So absorbed was she in her enjoyment of her feast, that she did not hear the door open and Mrs. Pennypoker come into the kitchen.

"Jane!" said the strong voice.

Janey started at the sound, and choked on a seed.

"Yes, mis'," she responded as soon as she could speak, while she raised her head from the rind.

"What are you doing?" demanded Mrs. Pennypoker sternly.

Her manner was not encouraging. There was a defiant flash in Janey's eyes, as she said sullenly,--

"Ol' mis' done got eyes. What she s'pose I's doin'?"

"But I told you to get the lunch."

"I was goin' to, in a minute; but Mars' Charlie done wanted me to cut his melon, an' I thought 'twouldn't make no difference."

"You are not here to think; you are here to do the work," said Mrs. Pennypoker magisterially. "If I tell you to do something, you must do it."

At the last words, Janey drew herself up to her full height and glared at Mrs. Pennypoker. Something in the unconscious dignity of her figure, as she stood there, seemed to dwarf her temporary mistress into insignificance.

"You cyarn' say mus' to me," she said in a slow, repressed tone. "Dese ain' no slave days, an ol' mis' cyarn' make 'em so. I ain' no heathen an' I ain' no slave. My mammy bought herself an' her husban', an' we's all freeborn."

She had moved forward a step or two, and thrown out her hand, while her eyes gleamed with an angry luster. Suddenly she controlled herself.

"I sha'n' say no mo'," she went on slowly; "'cause I might forget myself an' be sassy, an' I don' wan' to do dat. But ol' mis' better not interfere with me, an' say mus', or I'll pack my trunk an' not come back till Mrs. Burnam comes home. She buys my time, an' while I'm yere I belongs to her; but she don' bully me. *She's* a lady like what we use' ter have down Souf, befo' de war; not like you Yankees."

Into her final sentence Janey had compressed all the scorn of which she was capable. For a moment longer, she stood facing Mrs. Pennypoker; then, turning on her heel, she left the room.

Mrs. Pennypoker was the first one of the group to come to her senses.

"That girl shall leave the house to-night," she exclaimed angrily. "I won't have her here an hour longer."

"You aren't going to send Janey off!" demanded Allie indignantly.

"I certainly shall not keep her after what has occurred," returned Mrs. Pennypoker coldly.

"But you can't; she isn't yours. She's mamma's," remonstrated Allie.

"I am taking your mother's place for the present, and I shall not retain a servant who is so disrespectful," answered Mrs. Pennypoker again. "I am surprised at you, Alice, for interfering in a matter which does not belong to you."

"It does belong to me, too," returned Allie mutinously. "Janey's a splendid girl, and mamma just thinks everything of her. She'll never forgive you, if you send her off; and what's more, I hope she won't; so there, now!"

"Alice!" And there was no mistaking the meaning of Mrs. Pennypoker's tone.

"I don't care if 'tis!" exclaimed Allie, with illogical recklessness. "You're just too mean, and I don't blame Janey one bit."

"Alice!" repeated Mrs. Pennypoker. "You may go to your room, and not leave it again to-day. I shall tell your mother exactly what has occurred."

"Tell away!" returned Allie. "I just hope you will. I'm not afraid of mamma; she's not so cross as some people." And forcing back the angry tears, she walked away in the direction of her room, leaving the half-frightened boys to look alter her in silent sympathy.

Once in the safe retreat of her own room, Allie's courage broke down, and, throwing herself on her bed, she began to cry convulsively, as she realized all the injustice of her punishment, all the petty tyranny she had borne for the past three days. For a few moments the sobs came faster and faster. Then, when her first excitement was over, she began to think. Mrs. Pennypoker ought to be ashamed of herself for abusing them so; and how angry her mother would be when she knew it! Perhaps the long day of loneliness and fasting would make her ill; then Mrs. Pennypoker would be sorry. It might be that she would never get over it, but would go into a decline. How they would all mourn for her! She went on to plan the minutest details of her funeral with all the gloomy cheerfulness of an undertaker; but, when she came to fancy the loneliness of Howard and Charlie, the distressing picture overcame her, and she began to sob once more. However, the tears would not flow quite so readily this time; and, under all her pity for herself, she began to wonder uneasily if, perhaps, she had not been a little hasty and rude to Mrs. Pennypoker. It might be that her mother would not altogether sympathize with her, after all. This was not an agreeable thought, and, to silence it, she sprang up and crossed the room to put some cold water on her flushed and swollen face. As she did so, she saw a slip of paper tucked under the door, and she seized it eagerly, for it was addressed to her, and in Charlie's writing.

"Good for you, Allie!" it said. "Keep up your pluck till afternoon, and we'll have some fun then."

There was something encouraging in the boyish sympathy; and, as Allie stood caressingly rubbing the note against her cheek, she found herself wondering what he could mean by his reference to possible fun in the afternoon. The outlook for the rest of the day did not seem to promise much in the way of enjoyment; but Allie knew her cousin's ingenuity well enough to rely upon his word, so she could resign herself to wait.

The next hour was a long one to the young prisoner, who wandered restlessly about the room, or tried to amuse herself with a book, although all the time she was inwardly dwelling upon the ignominy of her punishment, and dreading lest it should reach the ears of Marjorie and the Everetts, or, worst of all, of Dr. Brownlee, whose good opinion she especially desired to retain. At the end of the hour, Mrs. Pennypoker herself appeared on the threshold, with a plate of crackers in one hand and a glass of water in the other. Without a word to the captive, she set the meagre lunch upon the table, and withdrew, locking the door behind her. At this last insult, Allie's temper flashed up again. It was enough to punish her so severely; but it was not necessary to distrust her honor, and lock her up like a criminal. At least, she would not touch the rations her jailer had left. Deliberately she picked them up, and, going to the window, she threw out the water with a splash, and tossed the crackers after it. She hesitated for a moment, and then hurled the plate and glass after them, with an angry determination which sent them crashing far across the uneven ground beneath her window. That done, she sat down to read with a quieted conscience.

Through the closed door she could hear Mrs. Pennypoker moving to and fro about the house, and now and again Vic's baby voice fell upon her ears; but, for the most part, the house was very still. At length she heard some one calling her name in a low voice. Throwing aside her book, she went to the door and listened intently, till she heard the call repeated. This time it was evident that the sound came from outside the window. She hurried across the room and threw it wide open. In a moment more Charlie had scrambled into the room.

"Hullo!" he remarked, as he tossed his cap into a chair. "You're awfully warm in here, so let's leave the window open. We're safe enough, for Mrs. Pennypoker can't hear us. Besides, Dr. Hornblower is in the parlor talking to her, and she won't know anything more to-day."

"But what are you going to do?" asked Allie, watching him in amazement, as he seated himself at his ease and unbuttoned his light gray coat, to expose to view a great round parcel concealed inside it.

"I'm going to spend the afternoon with you, of course," returned Charlie composedly. "You didn't s'pose I was going back on you after the way you stuck to me last June? Well, not much! We could climb out of the window and go off, but she'd be sure to find it out, and that would only make it worse, so we'll stay here and have a lark."

"You're a dear old boy, Charlie!" And Allie embraced him tempestuously. "But how did you ever stand it to be shut in here so long, last summer? This last hour has 'most killed me."

"I wasn't all alone, you know, much of the time. But, I say, come off!" he remonstrated, as Allie renewed her demonstrations of affection. "You needn't stand my hair on end just because I've come. Here's a pie I sniped off the pantry shelf, for I thought most likely you'd be hungry."

"I'm nearly starved," answered Allie gratefully. "Mrs. Pennypoker did bring me some crackers this noon, though."

"Crackers aren't much good, and those are all gone by this time, aren't they?" inquired Charlie scornfully.

"Yes, every one; gone out of the window," returned her cousin disdainfully. "Charlie MacGregor, I'd have starved to death before I touched one of her old crackers!"

"That's the way to talk," said Charlie approvingly. "She's a Tartar and a Turk, Allie, and I'd like to tell her what I think of her--if I only dared. But, if I did, she'd just lock us up in different rooms; and it's more fun to be together."

"I did tell her--Oh, dear, I wish mamma would come back," sighed Allie. "How shall we ever stand it three more days, Charlie?"

"Grin and bear it, mostly," returned Charlie, philosophically. "Janey's packed up her clothes and gone off, and she says she won't step into this house again till auntie gets back. I don't blame her; but Mrs. Pennypoker'll have to turn cook, or else send over for Wang. But go on and eat your pie, Allie, and you'll feel better. She's a Turk, I tell you; but I'll see that auntie knows all about it, and I know she won't think you're a bit to blame."

"But, Charlie, you aren't going to stay here all this everlasting afternoon," remonstrated Allie, as her woe yielded to the combined influences of her cousin's consolation and his pie. "It isn't fair at all, when you might be off with the boys having a good time."

"Well, it strikes me this ought to be my innings," answered Charlie quietly, while he settled his glasses on his nose and then took up the book which his cousin had just tossed aside. "How many days and weeks, I'd like to know, did you stay in here with me, when 't was hot and dark and stuffy here! It's only fair that you should let me take my turn now. You needn't talk to me, if you don't want to; but I shall stay here as long as I choose, and you can't put me out, so you may as well make up your mind to it."

Two hours later, as Mrs. Pennypoker's step was heard in the hall outside,

Charlie quietly let himself drop from the window-sill. Then he turned back to whisper,--

"Just don't you say anything about it, Allie; we aren't even now, and we sha'n't be, very soon. Besides, it's worth all the rest to have the fun of getting the inside track of her. Good-by till breakfast-time!" And he vanished around the corner of the house.

CHAPTER XIII.

AT THE NINE-HUNDRED LEVEL.

Late October had come, and already the snow-line was creeping down the mountain sides towards the little town in the cañon. Occasional flurries of snow filled the air, too, and the nights were sharp and frosty; but in the middle of the day it was still warm and bright, with a clearer, more bracing air than the summer had given, an air which tempted the young people out for long walks and rides up and down the valley. Louise often joined them in these expeditions, and it was no uncommon thing for them to be overtaken by Dr. Brownlee, who generally begged permission to spend a leisure hour with their party. This addition to their number was always hailed with delight by the children; for while the doctor usually took his place by the side of Louise, he was never too much absorbed in his companion to join the boys in their fun, or to treat Allie and Marjorie with the gentle chivalry which made them feel so grown up and elegant, a chivalry that is so rarely shown to children, yet never fails to afford them a delight even more keen than it gives to their older sisters.

Allie and the boys were coming up through the town, one Saturday morning, after a brisk walk in the clear, crisp air. They had passed "tin-can-dom," as Howard called the open field just below the town, which was thickly strewn with these indigestible relics of past feasts, and were just outside the fence separating Chinatown from its American surroundings, when Allie stopped abruptly.

"Look there!" she exclaimed, pointing over the low wall into the enclosure, where the tiny log cabins were scattered irregularly about the ground, and where long-tailed, moon-faced Chinamen were scuffling aimlessly about. "Isn't that Vic?"

"Where?" asked Howard, while Charlie added,--

"What an idea, Allie! Of course he wouldn't be in there."

"Yes; but 'tis Vic. I know that long red coat of his," responded Allie hastily. "Right in there, between those two log houses--see?"

True enough, there in the forbidden ground of Chinatown stood Vic, his red coat and fez making him a striking little figure against the dull background of a rough log house, as he gazed intently up into the yellow face of an elderly Chinaman, who was carrying two buckets of water hanging from a yoke across his shoulders.

"'Tis, after all; but what can he be doing there?" said Charlie, staring in astonishment at the scene before him.

"Never mind what he's doing," said Allie. "He ran away, I suppose; but we must get him home. I'll wait here, while you go and bring him out. Mamma'd be dreadfully frightened if she knew where he was. Now hurry!"

The boys dashed away, and soon came back to her side, with the small wanderer between them. Vic was in a state of open rebellion over this abrupt ending to his explorations, and lifted up his voice in lamentation, as Allie firmly turned his steps towards home.

"Everybody went off," he explained in an aggrieved tone. "You went, and Ben went, and papa went, and ven I went, too. And I will go back to see the Moolly-cow-man."

But his sister refused to be persuaded, and Vic's voice died away to a whisper, as he continued to babble to himself of the wonders he had seen in his walk.

"There's one thing, Allie, that I don't get used to, in this country," remarked Charlie, as they were crossing the main street; "and that's the signs. See there!" And he pointed to a long, white building, one door of which was surmounted with the sign, in great gilt letters: *Embalming Emporium*; while a board, swinging out from its next-door neighbor, bore the legend, *Shoos 1/2 Soled Here*. "But, I say," he added, as they came in sight of the house; "what do you suppose Ned and Grant want? They've camped out on our piazza, as if they meant to stay there. Hi--i!" he shouted, waving his cap above his head.

"Hurry u--up!" responded Ned, returning the salute with interest.

"Thought you'd never come," added Grant, as they drew nearer.

"What do you want?" asked Howard.

But before Ned had time to reply, Allie interposed,--

"Just wait one minute, do, till I take Vic into the house to mamma. Is she very much worried about him?"

"Don't believe she is," answered Ned. "She didn't say anything about it. Probably she hasn't missed him at all. Now," he resumed, as Allie came back to the piazza; "I've been waiting here for thirty-nine ages and a quarter; and I was just ready to give up and go home again. Papa sent me up to tell you that he's going to take a crowd down the Blue Creek, this afternoon, and to ask you if you don't want to come along with us."

"I shouldn't think he'd dare take Charlie again, for fear he'd hoodoo it all," said Grant disrespectfully.

"Who's going?" asked Howard.

"All of us; Cousin Euphemia and all; and Dr. Brownlee and Marjorie and you. We're going to have an early dinner, and start at one, so we can go through the smelter, after we come up. Cousin Euphemia is making her will now, most likely; she didn't want to go, but papa talked her into it. You'll be on hand; won't you?"

"We'll be thar," responded Howard, with a twang that might have done credit to Janey.

"Isn't it fun to go!" said Allie delightedly. "I've always wanted to go down, and never could. You and I will be the green ones, Charlie; all the rest have been before."

"The doctor and Cousin Euphemia haven't," said Ned. "But I'll take care of you, Allie, and show you all there is to be seen. Come along, Grant; we must be going." And the brothers departed in haste.

Punctually at one o'clock, Charlie and his cousins were at the Everetts', where they found that their party had received one unexpected addition. The Reverend Gabriel Hornblower had dropped in to dinner, and common courtesy had made it necessary for Mr. Everett to invite him to join the expedition. As they left the house, Louise, with her father and Dr. Brownlee, took the lead, while close in the rear walked Dr. Hornblower, edging forward as far as possible, in order to join in their conversation, with an utter disregard of Mrs. Pennypoker, who had attached herself to his side, and manifested every intention of maintaining her position. The short walk through the town was quickly taken; and it was still early in the afternoon when they stood beside the shaft. Mr. Somers, Mr. Everett's assistant, was waiting for them there; and, a few moments later, the new cage had come up the shaft, and halted to receive them.

"But what makes them call it a cage?" demanded Allie, eyeing with disfavor the pair of heavy platforms before her "I thought 'twould have openwork brass sides, like the elevators in Denver."

"And hot and cold water, and gas, and all the other modern improvements?" inquired Ned, as he helped himself to a pair of candles in their iron sockets, and passed one of them on to Allie. "Don't be a snob, Allie; you won't find much furniture down below."

"You take Mrs. Pennypoker and my daughter, with the gentlemen, on the upper deck, Somers," Mr. Everett was saying; "and I'll take these children in the lower, and look out for them there."

According to the usual method, the upper platform was brought to the level of the ground, to receive its freight, before the cage was raised the necessary seven feet, to allow Mr. Everett and the young people to step on the lower floor. Then they slowly sank away from the light, down, down, while Allie clutched Ned's protecting hand, and tried in vain to enjoy her novel ride. At length they came to a halt at a broad, square station, and the two decks of the cage were quickly unloaded.

"This is the nine-hundred level," Mr. Everett told them, as they stood grouped about him. "We have three more below,--they're one hundred feet apart, you know,--and we're still sinking the shaft. The cage in that next compartment is given up to the men who are doing the sinking."

"It's a rich vein, then, I take it," said Dr. Brownlee.

"A fine one, better than we supposed when we bought it. It dips down sharply to the east, and we cross it at the five-hundred, so we don't have to work so far in any one direction to strike it. You see, we run a cross-cut straight out from the shaft, till we hit the vein; then we turn both ways and run along through it; so, at every level, our workings are like a great T, with the stem growing larger with every hundred feet we go down."

"And this is how deep?" asked Louise.

"Nine hundred," repeated her father, while he hastily snatched Marjorie out of the path of an ore car, which came thundering down the cross-cut and turned abruptly into the station.

"It's a solemn thing to feel that you are nine hundred feet from the light," observed Mrs. Pennypoker, as she gathered her skirts more closely about her.

"Yes," responded the Reverend Gabriel, waving his right hand, lamp and all; "it reminds one of the mighty power of the earthquake, when it stoops to trample on a worm."

Then they were silent, as they followed Mr. Everett through the long gallery, pausing now and then near one of the electric lights that dotted the corridor, to listen to his off-hand explanations of the work below ground. Dr. Brownlee appeared to be especially interested in the subject.

"How do you get the ore on the cage?" he asked. "Do you run it on, car and all, or do you unload it?"

"How little these Eastern folks do know!" remarked the Reverend Gabriel, in an audible aside to Louise.

"Perhaps we should all be better off, if we knew more about it," she replied, with a touch of coldness in her tone, as she turned her back upon the Reverend Gabriel, and took her place at her father's side, where she met the amused glance of Dr. Brownlee, who had overhead both remarks.

"They signal the cage, and run the car on it," answered Mr. Everett. "We don't let but one man ring for the engineer. He has to stay near one of the stations, where he can hear; and when the miners want him, they go to the station and pound their signal on one of the water-pipes, for him to repeat. We had a green hand, though, that tried to improve on our plan, a few years ago. He attempted to catch the cage on the fly, as it went up past him; and he actually aimed the car at it, and ran it down."

"Did he hit it?" asked Charlie.

"Hardly," returned Mr. Everett, laughing. "The cage was too quick for him, and went on up; and both the car and the man fell clear to the bottom of the shaft."

"Oh-h!" And Marjorie's eyes grew round with horror. "I should think 'twould have hurt him awfully."

"Well, yes, Marjorie; I should have thought it would," said Howard, mimicking her tone, while the others joined in the laugh at her expense.

Then they went on to the end of the cross-cut, and, turning at a sharp angle, they came into the drift, the long gallery running through the vein. For some distance, the drift, like the cross-cut, was lined with timbers, then the lining ceased, as they neared the end of the drift, where the miners were hard at work, drilling for fresh blasts, or tearing out the ore loosened by the last explosion, and loading it into the little car which stood ready to be run down the track to the station. Seven feet above, so that the roof of the lower level formed the flooring of the next, was another short gallery, where the men were busy stoping, digging out the ore from the upper tier. Dingy and grimy as they were, it was fascinating to watch them, burrowing, like so many moles, in the depths of the earth. The visitors lingered to look at them until they were frightened away by the preparations for a blast; then they slowly made their way back to the station, pausing a moment to watch a loaded car, as it rolled from the rails to the polished steel flooring, and swung around the corner into position, to wait for the cage. Mr. Everett looked at his watch.

"I'm sorry to hurry you," he said; "but I think we ought to be going; don't you, Somers? It's change day; and at three the cages will be full."

"Change day!" remarked Charlie to his cousin, in an undertone; "what's that?"

"Hush!" she whispered. "Don't show Dr. Hornblower how little you know. Remember that you're from the East, too."

But Dr. Brownlee was animated by no such motives of prudence, and quietly asked for an explanation of the term.

"We have two sets of men," Mr. Everett answered. "The day shift goes on at seven, and works till half past five; and the night one comes on at seven in the evening, and stays till half past five in the morning. Of course that's harder on one set of men than the other, so, once in two weeks, we have what we call change day. The day shift goes on at seven, and works till three; then the night fellows come right on and stay till eleven; and the old day shift comes back at eleven. By the next morning, you see, their places are just changed, and the night men are working in the daytime. Now," he added, as he stepped to the shaft, to ring his own private signal; "we'll go up and take a look through the smelter before--Why, where are Mrs. Pennypoker and Dr. Hornblower?"

There was a startled pause. No one had seen the missing members of the party since they had left the head of the drift, although they had supposed them to be following close behind their companions. Turning, they looked back up the cross-cut, but there was no Mrs. Pennypoker in sight. It seemed impossible that they could have lost their way, in a long, straight corridor, less than ten feet wide; some accident must have befallen them. Worst of all, there was no time for delay; the cage had just come for them, and in the distance could be heard the steps of the approaching miners, as they came in for the change of shift.

"We mustn't keep the cage waiting for us, now," said Mr. Everett hastily. "You go up with the others, Somers, and I'll go back and look them up. They can't be far off."

Turning, he walked rapidly back up the cross-cut, expecting at every moment to meet the truants, so sure was he that they had only loitered along behind the others, absorbed in discussing the spiritual welfare of Wang Kum and his Mongolian brethren. It was not until he had turned into the drift, and paused to question a group of miners whom he met there, that he began to be seriously alarmed. The men had not seen Mrs. Pennypoker and her escort since they had all been together at the head of the drift. Mr. Everett felt no hesitation in accepting their statement, for, in their ignorance of the relationship between the superintendent and his cousin, the miners spoke of Mrs. Pennypoker's appearance in such unguarded terms as left him no room to doubt their knowledge of the person for whom he was seeking. However, he still kept on to the head of the drift, thinking it possible that they might be in some dark corner, though he could think of no reason which should tempt them to conceal themselves in any such fashion. But his quest was unavailing, and, facing about, he returned to the head of the cross-cut where he paused, uncertain what course to pursue. Then he opened his mouth and shouted their names, with the full power of his strong bass voice. The sound echoed up and down through the galleries and then died away, to be followed by a high-pitched feminine shriek.

The cry came from the opposite end of the drift from the one which they had been exploring, and Mr. Everett turned his steps in that direction. This end had been abandoned, some days before, in consequence of a serious leak in the pipes connecting with the pump; and it was now only lighted for a short distance beyond the mouth of the cross-cut. Now that the pump had ceased, the water had settled over the floor, to form a deep, thick clay which rendered progress slow and difficult. He had just passed the last electric light and was proceeding even more cautiously than before, when he came to an abrupt halt. The feeble glimmer of his miner's lamp had fallen upon a strange picture, and one whose meaning he was not slow to grasp.

At one side of the drift and leaning against the wall, stood Mrs. Pennypoker, with one foot drawn up under her, much in the attitude of a meditative hen. A few feet away from her, the doctor was bending forward, with his lamp extended in one hand, while with his other he held his cane, which he was poking about in the soft, sticky mud.

[Illustration: "His lamp extended in one hand, while with his other he held his cane, which he was poking about in the soft, sticky mud."]

"Well," said Mr. Everett at length, after he had watched them in silence, during some moments; "what are you doing here?"

The Reverend Gabriel and Mrs. Pennypoker both started guiltily. So interested had they been in their search, that they had been unconscious of Mr. Everett's approach until he stood before them. In her surprise, Mrs. Pennypoker came near losing her balance, and, to support herself, she put down her other foot. It was a shapely foot, and was covered with an immaculate white stocking, for Mrs. Pennypoker still adhered to some of the fashions of her far-off youth. Then the Reverend Gabriel answered.

"We inadvertently strayed from our way and came into this place, without realizing whither our steps were leading us," he said, while he continued to prod the mud before him; "and at length we fell, as you might observe, into the miry clay. I had just suggested the expediency of our return, when Mrs. Pennypoker--um--in short, met with an accident which unduly detained us and--ah, I have it!" he exclaimed triumphantly, as he carefully worked his stick put through the earth, and extended it in mid-air, with a shapeless, dripping mass hanging on its tip.

No further explanation was needed. Mrs. Pennypoker, as has been said, still clung to some of the fashions of bygone days; and, among other similar foibles, she cherished a fondness for congress gaiters, and invariably wore those feeble apologies for shoes whose limp cloth uppers are held in place by means of elastic wedges at the sides. In arraying herself for her visit to the mine, with characteristic New England thrift, she had put on an ancient pair of these gaiters, whose elastic sides had long since lost all their spring, and lay in ample folds about her ankles.

As Mr. Everett had surmised, his cousin, feeling no deep interest in the mine, had fallen into a theological discussion with her pastor. This had so engrossed them both that they had lost their way, and had only come to their senses when they found themselves in the dark, muddy passage of the deserted drift. They had hastily turned to retrace their steps, when Mrs. Pennypoker's foot slipped and plunged deep down into the clay; and, on her withdrawing it, she was horrified to feel that her foot was slowly but surely pulling out of her gaiter, instead of pulling her gaiter out with it. In vain she had attempted to work her foot down into her shoe once more; in vain she had endeavored to hook her bent toes into it, with a hold sufficient to draw it out. The mischief was done, and she could only lift up her foot, while the soft mud quickly settled in above the gaiter, and left no trace of the spot where it lay embedded.

It was evidently impossible for her to wade back to the cross-cut without it, and her size, age and dignity all combined to make it equally impossible for her to hop on one foot as far as the cross-cut; so she had been forced to come to a halt, while her companion prospected about in the earth, to find the vein in which his treasure was buried. At last it was found; but not even Mrs. Euphemia Pennypoker could present a dignified appearance as she received her muddy shoe from the end of the Reverend Gabriel's cane, drew it on to her foot, and walked away towards the station, with mingled clay and water oozing out from her gaiter, at her every step.

CHAPTER XIV.

THE BEGINNING OF THE OLD STORY.

Once more winter had come, and the snow lay deep and white over the little camp. The pines on the mountain sides looked a hazy blue against the glistening slopes, and the bald white summits of the mountains themselves stood out in bold relief against the clear blue heavens. Even the night sky was changed at that altitude, for the stars glittered down through the cold, still air, with an intensity which made them look like gleaming bits of metal scattered over the dense, dark-blue clouds; while often and often the north was lighted with the glare of the pale aurora which streamed far across the sky, in long, waving banners of rose color or light green.

"But I like the way you people out here make fun of New England weather," remonstrated Charlie one day, as he stood in the front window, watching a sudden flurry of snow sweep down through the cañon. "When I went down town to get the mail, this morning, it was raining so hard that I wore my mackintosh; but, by the time I was at the post-office, the sun was shining. I walked straight back home again, and it was hailing when I came up the steps. What sort of a climate do you call it, anyway?"

"A perfect one," returned Allie loyally.

"Not much! Montana buys up the job lots of weather left over from the other States, and cuts them up small before she serves them out again, just as they happen to come. Montana weather and Montana slang are the two richest crops in the State."

The past two months had been unbroken by any event of marked importance. Between their lessons and their frolics, the time of the young people had been well filled, and the days had hurried by, without any one's stopping to ask where they had gone. At the Burnams', life was going on smoothly and pleasantly, although Mr. Burnam was now busy in the field, hurrying to accomplish all that he could, before the storms of February should drive his party out of the mountains, until the spring thaws made field work possible once more.

By way of helping to pass the long winter evenings, Charlie had tried to bribe Allie to become his pupil and, after his hour of practice was ended, he usually took her in hand for a time, in a vain endeavor to teach her to play. But, in spite of her desire to please her cousin, Allie had neither the patience nor steadiness needful to keep her at the piano; and she much preferred to settle herself comfortably in front of the fire, and listen to her cousin's performances, rather than go through the drudgery of scales and exercises, upon which Charlie insisted, as the orthodox preparation for later work. Accordingly, Allie's music usually ended in a playful skirmish which sent Charlie back to the piano, to beguile her into good temper again, by means of some favorite melody. On rare occasions, when she was uncommonly meek, or when all other employment failed, she would be coaxed into running up and down over a few scales; but, in the end, her fingers invariably became snarled up with her thumbs; and, after one or two discordant crashes on the keys, she gave it up and threatened to buy a hand-organ for her contribution to the family music.

Her singing appeared to succeed no better. While she had a sweet, flexible voice, and went about the house singing softly to herself, as soon as she approached the piano a spirit of perversity seemed to enter into her, and she wandered along at her own sweet will, perfectly regardless of the time and key of the accompaniment with which Charlie was struggling to follow her. At length her cousin was forced to abandon his efforts and allow her to drop back into her old place as listener, a part which she always played with perfect success and contentment, while he turned his attention to the others. Grant was taking banjo lessons now, and Ned occasionally strummed a little on the venerable guitar which Louise had thrown aside in favor of her mandolin; so their little orchestra was frequently in demand to fill in gaps in an evening's entertainment. Howard and Marjorie, too, were ready to add their share of music, for they had toiled away in secret till they had mastered one or two simple duets, which they invariably sang whenever an opportunity offered.

In the mean time, a warm friendship had developed between Mr. Everett and Dr. Brownlee. The young doctor was now a frequent guest at the superintendent's house, where he had quickly become popular with them all, even to Mrs. Pennypoker, who never failed to array herself in her best gown and unbend her majesty whenever he was expected to appear. The acquaintance started during their camping expedition had rapidly ripened into a mutual liking, and it was surprising to see how often the younger man found time to drop in at Mr. Everett's office, late in the afternoon, for a few minutes' conversation. Once there, it was only natural that he should walk home with his friend, and, after a little polite hesitation, accept his invitation to come in for a call. Little by little the calls grew in length until, from accepting occasional invitations to dine, the doctor came to stay, quite as a matter of course, although he still made a feeble pretence of rising to go away, before yielding to their suggestion of dinner and a game of whist later on in the evening. At length, even this form was abandoned, and it grew to be an established fact that, whenever the doctor dropped in for an afternoon call, an extra plate and chair should be included in the dinner preparations, and that the card table should be brought out as soon as the meal was over. It also soon came to be a matter of course that Louise and the doctor should always play together, while

Mr. Everett and Mrs. Pennypoker ranged themselves against them, and devoted their attention to the game with unswerving vigilance. Not even Mrs. Pennypoker had been able to withstand the doctor's genial, hearty manner; and, in his presence, she laid aside her eye-glasses and her dignity, and laughed at all his jokes in an appreciative fashion, which Ned and Grant were quite at a loss to understand, since she never paid the slightest heed to their attempts at facetiousness.

In spite of the strict etiquette of the game which demands such perfect silence and watchfulness, it is strange how rapidly a newly-formed acquaintance can grow into strong friendship around a whist table. Everything conspires to help it on: the absorption of the opponents in their own hands; the chivalrous offer, on one side, to do all the dealing, and the grateful accepting of the courtesy on the other; and, most of all, the moment of hesitation over a doubtful play, followed by the silent meeting of the eyes, as the trick falls to one or the other. And yet, neither Louise nor Dr. Brownlee realized in the least whither they were so rapidly drifting. The doctor still regarded Mr. Everett as his chief friend in the family, and thankfully accepted his hospitality, which broke in so pleasantly upon his solitary life at the boarding-house, where the long table was presided over by his landlady, with her cap awry and her sleeves rolled to her elbows, while she gossiped volubly with her boarders, in the intervals of her skirmishes with the frowsy waiting maid. And Louise? She only knew that she enjoyed the society of the young doctor, just as her father and Mrs. Pennypoker appeared to enjoy it; but, all unconsciously to herself, her young life was rounding out with a new, sweet meaning; and the womanhood opening before her was daily gaining fresh inspiration and purpose, from the influence of the true, earnest manhood of their frequent guest.

But the time had slipped away and Christmas was at hand. The week before the festival found the young people much absorbed in a little entertainment, to be given for the benefit of some local charity, in which they were all to take a part. Mr. Nelson had started the project, and had called upon Dr. Brownlee and Louise to help him form and carry out his plans. After much discussion, it had been arranged to have an hour of music and readings, followed by a play in which the doctor and Louise, Charlie, Marjorie, and Allie should be the actors. The play was quickly chosen, a little French one which Louise had translated, and adapted to their meagre resources of costume and scenery; and the rehearsals had been going on for some weeks, until the success of the enterprise was sufficiently assured to allow them to announce their plans and decide upon the date. The dress rehearsal had been held before a select audience of fathers and mothers, who were hearty in their praises of the saucy maid and the irrepressible young brother, while they thoroughly enjoyed the spirited acting of Louise, who, in the person of the widowed mother, did all that lay in her power to thwart the flirtations between the doctor and Allie, until her efforts were set at naught by the disloyalty of her maid and the traditions of amateur acting, which demand a happy ending to every love affair.

The little hall was well filled, the next evening. Audiences in Blue Creek were often rather mixed; and, on this particular occasion, rich and poor, young and old, had gathered, to show their interest in a worthy cause, and their liking for the young actors, whose unvarying kindness and courtesy had made them favorites throughout the town. Even Janey's black face looked on from the background, while far at one side sat Wang Kum with two of his friends, whom he had persuaded to buy tickets, as a proof of their loyalty to Louise.

Behind the scenes there reigned the usual confusion, preparatory to the rising of the curtain. Moreover, in some quarters, there existed grave doubts of the curtain's being prevailed upon to rise at all, since, the night before, it had persistently stuck fast, at two feet from the floor. At length all was in readiness for the first part of the program, and Charlie had just stepped forward to make his bow, before seating himself at the piano, when the doctor hurriedly approached Louise.

"Can you spare me, for three quarters of an hour?" he asked. "I've just heard, by the merest chance, that the evening train is off the track, down in the cut below the station. The engine jumped the track, and pulled the baggage car after it; they both rolled over, and they say one man is hurt. Nobody has sent for me; but I'd like to just run down, and see if I can be of any use."

For a moment, Louise looked aghast at the idea of losing her chief actor and assistant. Then she said cordially,--

"Go, of course. We'll arrange to do without you, in some way."

The doctor's eyes thanked her; but he wasted no time in mere words, as he went on hastily,--

"I wouldn't say anything to the audience, for 'twould just break up the whole affair. If you'll put off my reading till just before your last duet with Charlie, I'll be here, unless there's serious trouble. If there is any reason that I can't come, I'll send word at once." And he was gone.

The program of the first part of the evening was drawing smoothly to its close. Charlie had delighted his audience with his playing, both alone and with the Everett boys; Howard and Marjorie had sung a new duet, which they had learned, in honor of the occasion; and Allie had convulsed her more critical hearers with a recitation, which she had rendered with an originality of tone and gesture that would have struck terror to the followers of Delsarte, even though it had won her the first encore of the evening. Then, after a moment's enjoyment of the continued applause which had followed her disappearance from the stage, she came back once more, and gave them "Aunt Tabitha." She threw herself into it with an abandonment of fun which, in itself, would have been enough to show her sympathy with the trend of the poem, while she could not forbear glaring defiantly down upon Mrs. Pennypoker's uplifted countenance, as she delivered herself of the closing lines, with a fervor that astonished her audience,--

"'But when to the altar a victim I go, Aunt Tabitha'll tell me *she* never did so.'"

And she swept off from the little stage, in a parting storm of cheers.

In the mean time, Louise had heard nothing from Dr. Brownlee; and she was beginning to grow uneasy, for the time for his reading was at hand, and the play was to follow it almost immediately. She was just resolving to give up all hope, and bring the entertainment to a hasty close, when she saw the doctor come hurrying in at the side door. She turned to Charlie MacGregor, who chanced to be standing near her.

"Will you help me out, Charlie?" she asked. "Go on again, and play--anything, I don't care what, just to give Dr. Brownlee time to get his breath."

"But strikes me they've had about all of me they can stand," demurred Charlie.

"Never mind if they have," said Louise. "There isn't anybody else that can appear, at a minute's warning. Go, please."

The next moment the doctor was by her side.

"Miss Everett, have you any powder?" he asked, laughing a little, as he pointed to a great purplish bruise on the side of his forehead.

"Dr. Brownlee!" she exclaimed in alarm. "What is it? Are you hurt?"

"Hush!" he said, in a low voice, though he was conscious of a quick sense of pleasure at the anxiety of her tone. "It's only a bump; but it doesn't look well, and I don't want it to show. Can't you cover it up somehow, before I go on?"

"Come this way," she said hastily. "I'm not much used to powder, but I'll see what I can do. Tell me," she begged, as the doctor dropped into a chair; "what has happened? It's a bad bruise, and your cheek is cut; what was it?"

"I was helping them get the man out of the car, and one of the beams fell against me; that's all. I found the new doctor, Dr. Hofer, in charge; so I just helped him lift the man out, and then came back here," he answered as lightly as he could, and without adding a word about the moments that he himself had lain there stunned from the force of the blow on his head.

Louise looked down at him anxiously. His face was white, and his hands were a little unsteady.

"Please don't try to read, Dr. Brownlee," she urged. "I'm sure you don't feel able."

"I'm all right," he said, rousing himself with a forced laugh; "if you can cover up the spot so it won't show. I don't want them to think I've been fighting."

He resigned himself into her hands, while she hunted among the properties for the powder-puff and the comb, and then did her best to conceal the great bruise on his temple, which had quickly swollen and turned dark. But, even as she did so, she felt a sudden impulse to drop the puff and run away, rather than meet the earnest gaze of the gray eyes looking so steadily up into her own, and listen to the quiet "Thank you," which greeted the end of the toilet, as the doctor rose and stepped forward to take his place on the stage.

At the suggestion of Mr. Nelson, he had decided to read "Elizabeth"; and Louise, as she stood at the side of the stage, listening to the quaint old tale of the Quaker wooing, found herself forgetting all her surroundings in the interest of the familiar story. Dr. Brownlee had turned a little to one side, in order to conceal his discolored temple from the audience, and this brought him into a position directly facing the young woman who, quite unconsciously, made a charming picture in the gown she had donned for the play. Just in the act of turning a leaf of the book in his hand, the doctor raised his eyes, and they rested upon her fair young face. As he did so, there rushed into his mind the memory of her womanly pity and gentleness in caring for his bruise, and he seemed to feel again the touch of her light hands upon his hair. He paused; then, with his gaze still fixed upon her, he went on in his quiet voice, low, but so distinct that not a syllable was lost on its hearers,--

"'I have something to tell thee, Not to be spoken lightly, nor in the presence of others. Them it concerneth not, only thee and me it concerneth.'"

Just then Louise raised her eyes to his; but, as she met the intentness of his look, her own eyes drooped, while the color rushed to her cheeks and then fled again. For a moment more the doctor's eyes rested upon her, then he went on with his reading; but his voice was unsteady and his heart was throbbing with the sudden new hope that had come to him.

The reading was ended, and the curtain fell amid the enthusiastic applause of the audience, who devoted the intermission to discussing the performers, with a perfect unconsciousness of the fact that two of them had entered upon a new life during the past hour. Though their secret was as yet unspoken, that one look had taught both Louise and Dr. Brownlee that the stories of their future lives were written in the same volume. Already they had glanced at the preface, and soon the first chapter would lie open in their hands.

But now there was no time for any such thoughts, for chaos once more reigned behind the scenes, as the actors hastily dressed for the play; and, within a few moments, the curtain rose again upon the transformed scene. Howard and the Everett boys, who had finished their share in the program, had come out into the audience in order to get a better view of the stage. After a little hesitation, they had discovered some vacant seats behind Wang Kum and his friends, who were sitting spellbound in their admiration of the scenes before them. For a time the boys listened attentively; but a constant attendance at the rehearsals had made the play an old story to them, and their interest began to flag. Grant was lazily leaning back in his seat, with one hand outstretched, abstractedly swinging Wang Kum's pigtail to and fro, when Ned suddenly started up, with a naughty sparkle in his dark eyes.

"Say, Howard, haven't you a piece of string in some of your pockets?" he whispered.

"I d'know," answered Howard, in the same stealthy tone. "What you want?"

Ned bent over to speak a few low words in his ear, and both the boys began to giggle.

"What's the joke?" inquired Grant curiously; while Howard dived into one pocket after another.

Ned cautiously imparted the secret to his brother, who received it with manifest delight; then he took possession of the dozen or more scraps of twine that Howard had produced, and tied them together to form one long string. This done, he appeared to lose all consciousness of the people around him, in the interest of the play, for he bent forward with his hands on his knees and stared fixedly at the stage. A moment later he drew a long breath and leaned back in his chair. Then it became apparent that his hands had not been idle, for one end of the string was securely tied about the tip of Wang Kum's queue, and woven in and out through the openwork back of his chair, while the rest of the string was in Howard's hands, to be passed on in turn to Grant. Five minutes afterwards the three unconscious Chinamen were firmly lashed to their seats and the boys had once more disappeared behind the scenes.

The play was at last ended, and the actors were called before the curtain for one final round of applause, in which the Chinamen joined with unflagging zeal. Then the audience rose to leave the hall, and the miners respectfully stood aside to let their superintendent and his party take the lead. Wang and his brethren still sat quiet, watching the people flock past them, with an evident determination to stay until the very end; but at length they too grasped their hats and started to rise. The next instant there was a clattering of chairs, followed by three startled howls, which broke upon the air and turned every face in the same direction. There in a row stood the three Chinamen, ruefully rubbing the backs of their heads, while their little almond eyes seemed to be popping out from their sockets, with surprise and with the unwonted strain upon their scalps. From the end of every pigtail dangled one of the light folding chairs which filled the room. Howard's strings were as strong as Ned's knots were firm. The Chinamen had not risen from their seats; their seats had risen with the Chinamen.

CHAPTER XV.

MR. ATHERDEN.

"Really and truly, Charlie, I never should have known you; you look so perfectly elegant."

"Thank you, ma'am!" And Charlie bowed low before his cousin, who joined him in the laugh at the unexpected form that her intended compliment had taken.

"You know what I mean," she said saucily. "Of course, you're always a dear old boy, even if you aren't a beauty. But now there's a sort of young man look to you, that makes me half afraid of you."

"Perhaps, if you stayed so, you'd treat me a little better," suggested Charlie teasingly. "I feel most uncommon queer, though. Do you honestly like the looks, Allie?"

Allie dropped into an easy-chair, and surveyed him from head to foot.

"Now turn around very slowly," she commanded; "and then walk off a few steps, so. Yes," she added, after an admiring pause; "you really do look very well, considering who you are; only I never, never should know you. It just changes you all over, and makes you seem four or five years older."

"Wish I were!" remarked Charlie meditatively. "Only I should be ready for college then, and have to go back East and leave you. What a jolly year this has been!"

"Yes, it has," assented Allie absently. She was still looking up at her cousin, with a feeling of sisterly pride in the tall, straight figure before her.

Montana had evidently agreed with the boy, for, during the year he had spent there, he had grown so rapidly as to leave Howard far below him. Contrary to the custom of most boys, he bore his added inches with perfect ease, and had entirely escaped the stage of awkward consciousness, which falls to the lot of nearly all growing lads. Even now, young as he was, there was a quiet dignity in his manner which, combined with his manly figure, made it seem high time that he should take the first marked step towards man's estate, and leave off knickerbockers. The new suit, ordered from New York, had come that day; and

Charlie had dressed himself up in it, and appeared before Allie, to demand her respectful attention.

Had Charlie attired himself in a checked apron and sunbonnet, it would have seemed a thoroughly admirable costume to his cousin's eyes; but, on this particular evening, Allie's praise was well-merited, for the new suit was unmistakably a success. Charlie was one of those few, but fortunate boys who can wear even shabby clothes with an air that gives them a certain elegance; and he had grace enough to enable him to escape the usual awkwardness, which comes to the young girl in managing her first train, to the boy in appearing in his first long suit. As Allie had said it made him look much older and more dignified, until she almost felt that she had lost her jovial playfellow, and stood in the presence of a fine young man. Still, she liked the change, as long as it really was the same old Charlie; and she continued to watch him, while a little contented smile gathered about the corners of her mouth.

"Yes," she repeated; "I should hardly have known you. Come here a minute, and I can change you so you wouldn't recognize yourself a bit."

Charlie laughed at the seriousness of her tone, as he seated himself on the arm of her chair, while she patted and poked at his hair, until she had parted it in the middle and brushed it away from his forehead, where it usually lay in a close, short fringe. She studied the effect for a moment; then she gently pulled off his glasses.

"Poor old boy!" she said caressingly, as she drew her finger down along the narrow white scar that crossed his upper lid. "You still carry your beauty-spot; don't you? I wish 'twould go away."

"What for? Does it show so very much?" asked Charlie.

"No, not a bit, with your glasses on; but I never like to think back to that horrid day," she replied, with a frown. "I was sure you were going to die, or something."

"Well, I didn't. You see, I'm tough," returned Charlie placidly. "Besides, we had some good fun together, after the first week or two. But how do you like the looks?"

"Your own great-grandmother wouldn't have any idea who you were," said Allie decidedly.

"Most likely not," observed Charlie.

"But just you go and look in the glass, and see for yourself!" And Allie sprang up, and dragged her cousin to the nearest mirror. All at once she began to caper madly about the room.

"What's struck you, Allie?" inquired Charlie, pausing in his contemplation of himself to stare at his excited cousin.

"I've just had the most lovely idea," said Allie incoherently. "It's too much fun for anything, and we must do it."

"Do what?"

"Well, now you see here," she was beginning, with sudden solemnity, when her cousin interrupted her,--

"Give me my glasses, then."

"Yes, I know that; but listen! Don't you wear your suit again this week, nor tell anybody you have it, and don't let Howard tell, either. Next Tuesday is Mrs. Fisher's 'At Home,' you know; and we'll dress you up, and you can go over there, and everybody will take you for a strange young man. Won't it be fun?"

"Fine!" responded Charlie, as he led the way back to the parlor, and took his favorite position, leaning against the mantel. "Only I'm afraid everybody'd know me."

"Truly they wouldn't," answered Allie. "Can't you buy a mustache down at Bright's? That would finish it all up, and nobody would ever have any idea who you are. You're as tall as papa is, now."

"Well, I'll think about it," said Charlie. "I'm a little bit afraid to try, only it would be such immense fun. You keep mum about it, though, and maybe we can put it through."

Allie carried her point; and, directly after dinner, the next Tuesday evening, Howard was solemnly warned not to go near his room. A little later Allie knocked at the door and was admitted. Just across the threshold, she stopped in surprise and delight, as she caught sight of the elegant young man who rose to meet her.

"How perfectly splendid!" she exclaimed. "Where did you ever get such a mustache? It just matches your hair, and looks as if it must grow on."

"Hope I don't lose it off!" returned Charlie fervently, as he rendered himself temporarily cross-eyed, in his efforts to catch a glimpse of the silky thatch on his upper lip. "But I wish you'd take my hair in hand, Allie; it's so used to a bang, that it just won't stay parted."

"Let me try." And Allie took the comb, and devoted herself to coaxing her cousin's refractory locks to lie in the desired position. "It wants to be just in the middle, for you're going to be the dearest little dudelet you ever saw. Now take off your glasses."

"Oh, I must have those," remonstrated Charlie. "I'm blind as a bat without them, and I shall be sure to run into something, and tip it over."

"No, you won't," said Allie composedly. "If you wear them, people will be sure to know you."

"But, if I take them off, my scar will show," argued Charlie; "and that will give it all away. But, I say, I have some eye-glasses somewhere, that the oculist gave me, to start with. I don't ever wear them, 'cause they wouldn't stick to my nose. I lost them off into the soup, the first night at dinner, and I bought my spectacles early the next morning; but perhaps I can keep them on now."

"I should think you ought to; your nose is large enough," remarked Allie, with calm disrespect. "But get them; I can tell better when I see them."

There was an interval of silence, while Charlie rummaged in his bureau drawers. At length he unearthed the little case from a box containing an odd assortment of light hardware, broken knives, stray nails, an awl or two, and a collection of trout reels and flies.

"Here 'tis," he said. "I remember now; I used it to wind my best line on. How will they go?" And he turned to face his cousin, with a conscious laugh which promptly dislodged the glasses from his nose.

"That's better," said Allie approvingly; "they don't look a bit the same. I don't like them as well as I do the spectacles, for all the time; but they change you more. Now remember to be very easy and elegant, and don't act shy. Behave as if you thought you were very good to speak to them, and they'll like you all the better. And be sure you don't go too early."

"But what are you going to do now?" demanded Charlie, as she turned to the door. "You aren't going to be mean enough to leave me here all alone, till it's time to go?"

"I'm going to dress me," returned Allie. "I begged an invitation from Marjorie, and I'm going over there with mamma. You don't suppose that I'm going to lose all the fun, do you?" And she departed.

Society in Blue Creek was by no means as simple as a stranger might have been led to expect. During the winter months, there were few evenings that were not given up to some entertainment; and the little set to which the Burnams and Fishers and Everetts belonged were the gayest of the gay, with dinner parties and impromptu dances following one another in rapid succession. The enjoyment of these festivities was in no wise marred by the fact that one always met exactly the same people. Though the resources of the camp were not great, yet this set of friends was a thoroughly congenial one, consisting, as it did, of a dozen or more young married couples, together with several stray bachelors and a very few older people. Young women were deplorably scarce in Blue Creek, and, for a year, Louise had been the acknowledged belle among them, as she would have been, however, in the face of many rivals. Strangers, who were attracted to her side by her beauty, remained there, charmed by her easy manners and her ready wit; so, wherever she went she was sure to be the central figure of a little group of admirers, of whom Dr. Brownlee was usually the one nearest her side.

According to one of the pleasant customs of the little town, Mrs. Fisher had her weekly reception day. On Tuesday evenings, her house was always filled with the friends whom, with rare tact, she left to entertain themselves, while she moved up and down her charming rooms, with a word to one and a smile for another, now breaking in upon a flirtation which threatened to last too long, now bringing stray wallflowers into the middle of some hospitable group, and never for an instant forgetting to keep a watchful eye over any stranger who might chance to be among her guests. There was an attractive informality about these evenings, when one was at liberty to appear in a street gown, or an evening costume, and where the little supper was so simple as merely to be a pleasant break in the midst of the dancing, but not to suggest the idea of an overburdened hostess, struggling to feed a ravenous multitude. No one else in the town had quite the same gift for entertaining as Mrs. Fisher; no one else could carry out an "At Home" with quite such delightful simplicity. She gave them the use of her house, together with a cordial, unaffected welcome, and she left the rest to take care of itself. With this happy talent for receiving her friends, it was not strange that the tall, blonde woman was one of the most popular matrons in the camp.

This Tuesday evening was bidding fair to be as pleasant as its predecessors had been. The rooms were filled, and the air was echoing with the soft buzz of voices. A little pause in the dancing had scattered the young people, who were wandering about, some in the back parlor, watching the older guests grouped about the whist tables, some in the "den," across the hall, where the only light came from the great blazing fire which flickered over the pictures on the walls, and over the easy-chairs scattered about the cosy room. At the very back of the broad hall sat Louise and Dr. Brownlee, resting after their waltz, while they talked of one thing and another, the every-day interests which they shared in common. All at once Mrs. Fisher stood before them, with a young man at her side.

"I have been looking for you, Louise," she said. "Here is some one that I want to introduce to you: Mr. Atherden, Miss Everett. Mr. Atherden is a stranger, Miss Everett," she added; "and I leave it to you to make him feel at home. Dr. Brownlee, I wish you'd come and play the agreeable to Mrs. Nelson; she is looking dreadfully bored." And she led him away towards the parlor.

As Louise glanced up, at the introduction, she had been attracted by the young stranger before her. He was a man of about her own age, apparently, not very tall, but with a proud, erect carriage and a simple dignity which gave him the look of being a much larger man. His face, in spite of his eye-glasses and his silky, brown mustache, was almost boyish in its outlines; and he was faultlessly dressed, from his white tie and the white carnation in his button-hole, down to the toes of his shining shoes. His whole appearance was so likable that Louise welcomed him cordially, in spite of her regret at losing the doctor's society, and at once set about making him feel at home.

"How long have you been in Blue Creek, Mr. Atherden?" she asked politely. "I don't remember meeting you before."

"I only came a week ago," replied Mr. Atherden, as he took possession of the chair which Dr. Brownlee had so lately quitted. "I've been in San Francisco, the last two or three years; but I came up here to see about"--He hesitated for an instant; then he went on, with a little laugh. "Well, the fact is, I came up here to open an office. I'm a doctor, you know, and I heard that you hadn't a very good one here, and that there was a possible opening for another man."

"Indeed?" Louise's tone was icy in its politeness.

"Yes," resumed the young man, eyeing her closely; "so I thought I'd run up here and see for myself; but I found a first-rate man was in ahead of me, so I must depart in search of a fresh field."

"Then you are not to stay long?" said Louise, as she smiled on him with all her former kindness. "Blue Creek is really a pleasant place when you are used to it. You are unfortunate in seeing it at this season."

Her companion made some light answer, and they went on chatting like a pair of old friends. Louise was soon delighted to find that the stranger cared for music as much as she did, and was familiar with the best works of the masters, while he showed a thorough acquaintance with New York and its surroundings which was remarkable in a man who professed to have spent his life in California. There was something indescribably charming in his quiet ease of manner and in his boyish fun; and Louise found herself thoroughly enjoying their pleasant, off-hand conversation, though all the time she was conscious of a hazy resemblance to some one whom she had met before. Moved by this uncertain idea, she studied him closely, while in her own mind she went over and over her list of acquaintances, trying to find the person of whom she was thinking. Nor could she tell wherein the resemblance lay, whether in the voice, the manner, or in some feature; and yet it was there all the time, a fleeting, haunting likeness to some former friend. Then she thought she had a clue, for, in answer to a sudden jest on her part, the stranger laughed until his glasses fell off and dropped to the floor, and as he stooped to pick them up, she caught sight of a tiny scar on his right eyelid. Surely she had seen that scar before, or, at least, one much like it; and once more she went through her friends, trying to place the mark, but with no better success than before.

For a long half hour they sat there, while Mr. Atherden entertained her so well that she was quite unconscious of Dr. Brownlee, who came to the parlor door more than once to cast a longing glance in her direction. But her back was turned towards him, and she was too much interested in their talk to heed the proudly defiant glance with which Mr. Atherden met the gaze of his rival. The doctor was not so slow to interpret his meaning, and he gave his mustache a vicious jerk, as he walked away to pay his homage at some other shrine. Mr. Atherden watched him with an amused smile; then he turned to Allie who stood before him with a plate of sandwiches in her hand.

"Ah, thank you, my little maid," he said with infinite condescension, while he helped Louise and then himself. "Mrs. Fisher is to be congratulated upon having such charming assistants." And he looked straight up into the eyes of Allie, who flushed a rosy red as she hurriedly turned away.

But supper was over, and the tempting notes of a waltz rang out from the piano in the parlor. Mr. Atherden rose to his feet.

"It is a long time since I have danced, Miss Everett; may I not have the pleasure now?" And settling his glasses firmly on his nose, he smiled invitingly down at her, as he stood waiting to lead her to the parlor.

Louise hesitated for a moment. The doctor had asked her for this very waltz; but already the room was full of moving couples, and she could see him dancing with the pretty young teacher, lately come from the East. With a little feeling of pique she turned to her escort, and was soon gliding about the room with an apparent delight in her partner, who was dancing quite as well as he had talked. The waltz ended, she turned away, without a glance at the neglectful doctor, and followed her new acquaintance to their former seats in the hall.

"How well you waltz!" she said frankly, as she fanned herself. "It's such a rare thing to meet a really good dancer out here."

"Such a partner would inspire anyone," returned her companion gallantly, while he twirled his mustache with a complacent delight in it which convinced Louise that it was of recent growth.

Then he entered into a spirited account of his journey and his adventures in coming into the strange place, while Louise sat leaning back in her chair, watching him, haunted by that vague resemblance. Dr. Brownlee was standing just inside the parlor door with his eyes fixed upon them longingly, although he was apparently engrossed by the sprightly conversation of his former partner. But Mr. Atherden made no motion as if to leave his place; he merely glared defiantly at the doctor, while he twisted his mustache and chatted on, and the doctor was forced to go away again.

Notwithstanding her apparent unconsciousness of his presence, Louise had looked after him with a little wistful expression in her blue eyes. At that moment, she heard a sudden exclamation, and she turned back to face her companion once more, just in time to see the silky brown mustache yield to too violent a jerk and fall into his lap, while the young man, in no wise embarrassed by the accident, leaned back in his chair and burst into a shout of laughter. One glance at him had told her the secret of the puzzling resemblance; and she echoed his laugh with a thorough enjoyment of the boyish caper.

"Charlie MacGregor, you incorrigible imp!" she exclaimed, when she could get her breath. "How did you ever dare to come here in this fashion?"

"Why not?" inquired Charlie. "You'd never have known me now, if this miserable mustache had only stuck where it belonged. But, honestly, Miss Lou, don't I make a fair actor?"

"Too good, Charlie," she answered, with a fresh laugh over the unexpected ending to her flirtation. "Why haven't you ever told us you could waltz so well, though?"

"I didn't suppose I could; it's so long since I've tried it. Besides, none of the other fellows do, and I was afraid they'd think 'twas silly for a boy," answered Charlie. "Allie started this scheme, and put on the finishing touches. But didn't you really know me, Miss Lou?"

"Not a bit. Nobody would ever have suspected, if you hadn't been quite so proud of your mustache, Mr. Atherden. By the way, where did you get the name?"

"It's my middle one; didn't you know that?"

"No; but," she added hastily, "here comes somebody. Really, Charlie, you don't want to spoil the joke by getting caught; you'd better go, now." And she pushed him towards the door.

Five minutes later, she was offering to Mrs. Fisher the apologies of her stranger guest, for the sudden business which had called him away so abruptly. Then, after an inviting glance which promptly brought the doctor to her side, she led the way to the "den," where she pledged him to secrecy, and then told him the story of her recent companion.

"But there's one sure thing," Charlie said, with impenitent glee, as he was bidding Allie goodnight; "for once in my life, I cut Dr. Brownlee out with Miss Lou, and that's something to be proud of."

CHAPTER XVI.

THE COMPLETED STORY.

"They say there's a case of scarlet fever over the other side of the creek," remarked Mr. Everett at dinner, one night about a month after Charlie's unexpected appearance in society.

"Scarlet fever! Oh, dear, where?" asked Louise anxiously.

"You needn't be scared, Lou; people don't catch it at your age," responded Grant, with brotherly impertinence.

"I'm not afraid for myself," she answered seriously. "Where is it, papa? I don't want the boys to get into it."

"It's way up beyond the smelter," replied Mr. Everett lightly. "You don't need to worry, Lou, for it is so far away, and only a light case. The boys would better not go over that way, and then they'll be safe enough. Dr. Hofer has it in charge, so it will probably be all right."

"I suppose so; but I'm always afraid of it," said Louise uneasily. "I hope they'll quarantine them, or something."

"Of course they will," said her father. "No doctor that's half a doctor would let such a matter go unguarded. The board of health wouldn't allow it, either," he added, in a tone of such decision that Louise accepted his belief as final, and thought no more about the matter.

Ten days later she stood before her mirror, dressing for a *Mardi gras* party at the Fishers'. For the past three weeks, this coming social event had been the chief theme of conversation in Blue Creek; for, taking place, as it did, at the very close of the season, it was intended to be a fitting climax to all the gayety which had gone before. Louise had entered into the spirit of the occasion as heartily as a young and pretty girl could do, and had spent long hours in planning the new gown which her father had insisted she must have.

"Something simple and pretty, Lou; but good of its kind," had been his only instruction. "Don't spoil it, for the sake of a few dollars; just get something that can stand on its own merits, and not have to be patched out with laces and ribbons and all sorts of other gimcrackery. You know what I mean; but I want my daughter to look her best."

Nevertheless, after all her anticipations, Louise was looking a little troubled and anxious, as she stood there, arraying herself in the pale blue crape gown which fell about her in soft, clinging folds, unbroken by any ornament except the crescent of pearls that fastened the high, close ruff at her neck. For some reason, Ned had been feeling ill that day. He had complained of being cold, in the morning; and, instead of going to Mr. Nelson's as usual, he had lain on the sofa all day long, too miserable even to go with Grant to the Burnams', where the boys had been asked to spend the afternoon and dine. For the past day or two, Mr. Everett had been away from home on business, and would only return just in time to take his daughter to the Fishers'; and Mrs. Pennypoker had made light of the boy's trouble, pronouncing it merely a slight fit of indigestion which would be gone by the next morning. Still, Louise had been alarmed, unnecessarily so, Mrs. Pennypoker had told her. But the boy seemed thoroughly ill and feverish, and she had persuaded him to go to bed early, promising to hurry her dressing, and go in to sit with him until the carriage came for her.

Now, as she arranged her great bunch of white roses, and tied them with a long blue ribbon, before laying them ready beside her fan and gloves, she was half resolving to give up the party and stay quietly at home with Ned. Of the two boys, he was decidedly her favorite; and she disliked the idea of leaving him to the mercies of Mrs. Pennypoker, whose tenderness was a little too brazen in its nature to be acceptable to an affectionate, impressionable lad like Ned. However, she knew that her father was hurrying his return on purpose to act as her escort, so she was unwilling to disappoint him at the last moment. She was still hesitating what course to pursue, as she gathered up her train and started for her brother's room, with the largest of the roses in her hand, to leave with him when she went away. But, as soon as she came in sight of Ned's face, she felt no further doubt. Unaccustomed to illness as she was, she saw at a glance that the boy was worse, although he opened his eyes and smiled at her approvingly as she paused beside him.

"You look just gay," he said hoarsely.

"Gayer than you feel?" Louise asked playfully, while she bent over him and laid her cool hand against his flushed cheek.

"I'm all right; only I'm so warm, and my throat's a good deal sore," Ned answered; then he settled back under the blankets, and closed his eyes again.

Louise watched him closely for a moment. In spite of Mrs. Pennypoker's assurances, this was not like any form of indigestion she had ever seen, and she determined to send Wang Kum for Dr. Brownlee. From past experience, she knew that Mrs. Pennypoker would object to such a course, for she had unlimited faith in her stock of home medicines, and regarded the professional services of a doctor as invariably leading to the gloomy ministrations of the undertaker. Mrs. Pennypoker had never quite forgiven Mrs. Burnam for disregarding the poultice she had prescribed for Charlie's eye; and now, all day long, she had been persecuting Ned with alternate doses of ginger tea and "boneset bitters," which were her staple remedies for almost every ill to which flesh was heir. Louise had submitted, much against her better judgment; but now she felt that the time had come for decided action, so she stealthily made her way to the kitchen in search of Wang Kum.

"I wish you'd go over and ask Dr. Brownlee to come in here for a few minutes, as soon as he can, Wang," she said, in a low voice.

Wang Kum nodded wisely.

"All light; Wang sabe. You no wan' Mis' Pen'plok know." And he departed on his errand.

Quarter of an hour later the doctor came. Wang had interrupted him in the midst of dressing for the party, and he had hastily finished his toilet and hurried over to the Everetts, rather at a loss to account for the summons. Louise met him at the door.

"Dr. Brownlee!" she exclaimed, with an accent of relief; "it seemed as if you'd never come."

The doctor looked at her in surprise. From Wang's unconcerned manner, he had supposed that his message was in some way connected with the coming party; but the girl's pale, anxious face showed that there was some more serious cause for her sending to him. And yet he was only a human man; and, in spite of his quick sympathy for her unknown trouble, he paused for a moment to gaze at her admiringly, as she stood there with her long, light gown sweeping about her feet, and one hand stretched out to welcome him, while in the other she still held the great white rose that she had taken from the bunch he had sent her. Then the instinct of the doctor came uppermost once more.

"Is some one ill?" he asked briefly.

"Yes; it's Ned," answered Louise hurriedly. "He hasn't been well all day, and he's worse to-night, so I wanted you to see him. Cousin Euphemia says it's nothing but--Come, you can see for yourself."

In a moment more they were leaning over Ned, their evening costumes contrasting strangely with the flushed face of the restless little patient. With his usual bright, off-hand manner, the doctor greeted Ned, as if his coming had been simply a matter of chance. But he took careful note of his pulse and temperature, and asked a short, direct question or two; then, after a few words more, he left the room, beckoning to Louise to follow him.

"I'm glad you sent to me without waiting any longer, Miss Everett," he told her, as soon as they were in the parlor once more "We're going to have a case of scarlet fever in there, and it's high time some one was looking out for it."

"Scarlet fever--Ned have scarlet fever!" repeated his sister slowly, as she dropped into a chair. "Do you really mean it, Dr. Brownlee? Is he very ill?"

"Not yet," returned the doctor. "But, first of all, where is Grant? We must keep him out of the way."

"He's at the Burnams'," answered Louise, rising and walking nervously about the room.

"Well, send Wang over, and have Grant stay there. Mrs. Burnam will be willing to look out for him, I know; and he isn't likely to give them any exposure,--the mischief would be done by this time, anyway. And then you ought to go to--"

"I shall not go anywhere," she answered decidedly.

"But, Miss Everett, think of the danger of your taking the fever. I shall have to quarantine the house, too; and Mrs. Pennypoker will be here to take care of Ned."

Louise stopped in her restless walk, and turned to face the doctor, with her head raised proudly and a scornful curve to her lips.

"Dr. Brownlee, do you think that I am a coward?" she asked with cutting emphasis. "Ned may be very ill, and I could never leave him with Cousin Euphemia."

"But the danger," he urged again feebly, although he felt that her decision was the right one, and he admired her for it, even while he shrank from the thought of her possible peril.

Louise looked steadily into his eyes.

"Ned is my brother," she said firmly, though her lips were quivering; "and it is my right to stay. Besides, if anything should happen"--She paused abruptly, while the tears rushed to her eyes.

"Just as you think best," said the doctor gently. "You are needlessly alarmed to-night, Miss Everett. I will tell you the exact truth: Ned is a very sick boy, but there is no present danger for him. I needn't say that I shall do all I can to make it easier for you, but"--he hesitated; then added, with one of his cheery laughs, "The fact is, I'm most awfully glad that you insist on staying. Mrs. Pennypoker is a good woman; but she's no nurse, and Ned needs somebody that's a little less like a steam saw-mill, if he is going to be ill for a week or so. Now, I'll go down and get a prescription or two put up, and stop to see Mrs. Burnam about Grant's staying there, and then I'll be back again."

"But is it necessary?" remonstrated Louise, although she felt the support of his presence, and was grateful for it. "Papa will be here soon, or Wang can go; and you were going to the Fishers."

"The Fishers can get along without either of us to-night," he said laughingly. "We'll have our party here; we seem to be all ready for it." And he smiled meaningly at her dainty gown.

The door closed behind him, and Louise went quietly to her room, to take off her gown and put on a soft white wrapper, before going back to her brother. From the first, she had been sure, from the doctor's manner, that he had felt alarmed about Ned; but, in her present mood, she was grateful to him for his assumed carelessness, and she appreciated the kindness with which he was giving up the evening to her needs. Some sudden girlish regret made her snatch up the roses and bury her face in them, as two great tears rolled down her cheeks; then she quickly untied the flowers and put them back into the bowl, all but one, which she fastened in her gown, to be her companion and comfort in her long, anxious evening.

Early the next morning Dr. Brownlee was there again; and for the next week he was constant in his attendance, for the boy was very, very ill. Day after day the fever had increased, until it seemed as if the young, strong life must yield to its power. Now he lay in a heavy stupor, now he muttered and laughed to himself in wild delirium; but each night found him a little weaker than he had been the night before, and each morning brought from the doctor's lips the same sad verdict, "No better." During all these long days, Louise had scarcely left the room, but watched over him, night and day, with a fierceness of devotion which resented any interference.

"He's mine, I tell you," she said, turning on the doctor, who was trying to coax her from the room. "He's my brother and my favorite--oh, why can't you understand? He keeps calling me, when he doesn't know anybody else; and what if he should come to himself and want me, and I shouldn't be there? Let me stay with him while I can, for it may not be so very long--Oh, my Ned!" And brushing away the hot tears, she turned and went back to her old place.

Two days later the doctor slowly went up the steps to the door. His heart was heavy with dread, for he knew that the crisis was at hand, and he felt that the issue was more than doubtful. Without ringing the bell for Wang Kum to admit him, he entered the house, and went directly to Ned's room. He was in there for a long time; then he left Mr. Everett and Mrs. Pennypoker with the boy, and came out into the hall again. As he passed the parlor door, he paused for a moment; then he pushed it open, and went into the room. Beside the table sat Louise, with her head resting upon her folded arms, so still that he thought she must have fallen asleep from sheer exhaustion. But, as she heard his step she raised her head to speak to him, and he was shocked to see the hard, drawn lines on her pale face, and the dull, cold light in her eyes.

"They say it can't last much longer," she said wearily, and without asking him for his opinion.

"No," he assented gently, as he sat down by her side. "It can't be like this long; the change will come in a few hours, and then I hope our Ned will be better."

But Louise shook her head.

"What's the use of saying that, Dr. Brownlee?" she said, in a low, strained voice. "You don't mean it, I know; and I'm not a baby, to be comforted with just words. Oh, doctor, if I could only cry! I've tried to, and I can't,--can't do anything but think, and wonder what I shall do without Ned."

She was silent for a moment; then she went on excitedly, "Dr. Brownlee, if Ned doesn't get well, I shall always believe that Dr. Hofer killed him. There was a case of fever across the creek, and he let the children from that very house go all over town. One of them was in the choir, a week before Ned was taken ill. It was wicked, wicked! I can't have Ned's life thrown away, just for that. It mustn't be so; I can't bear it!" And her head dropped again, as she wailed, "Oh, doctor, can't you save him?"

The sight of her bitter sorrow was more than the doctor could bear, and his own voice was unsteady, as he answered sadly,--

"I will do what I can; but we can only wait and hope." He paused; then he laid one of his firm hands on hers, and said in a low voice, "Louise, I can't help you; but won't you give me the right to comfort you, to"--

But Louise interrupted him.

"Wait," she begged. "I can't think of it now--of anything but Ned. I must go back to him." And she left him alone.

Late that evening, the doctor and Mrs. Pennypoker sat by the bed, almost breathlessly watching the boy, who lay in a sort of stupor. Dr. Brownlee had come in early, and announced his intention of spending the night in the house, to watch over his patient. He had sent away Louise and her father to take a little rest, promising to call them, in case of any change. For more than two hours he had been sitting there, expecting the end to come at almost any moment; but still the boy's lethargy was unbroken.

Then, all at once, the doctor leaned forward and gazed closely at the face before him. The change had come, and Ned lay breathing quietly, in the longed-for, life-giving sleep. For a few moments more Dr. Brownlee sat there, scarcely daring to move; then, with a happy nod to Mrs. Pennypoker, he left her to wipe her eyes unseen, and stole away to tell the glad news to Louise.

He found her in the parlor, in her old position by the table, too much absorbed with her dread and sorrow to hear his step, until he was close at her side. She started up, with the question on her lips; but before she could speak the words, a glance at his face had told her all. With one little glad outcry, she seized his outstretched hand; then she dropped down on the sofa, to hide her face in the pillows and sob like a little child, in all the fervor of her joy and thankfulness.

The doctor stood waiting by her side, until her first outburst was over; then, when she had grown more quiet, he bent down beside her, to say gently,--

"And now, Louise"--

There was no need for many words. For an instant, Louise looked up into the expectant face above her; then she put her hand in his.

CHAPTER XVII.

THE TRAGEDY OF THE UNEXPECTED.

"Did you get any letters this morning, Wang?" inquired Mrs. Pennypoker, as the Chinaman came in to remove the dishes from the breakfast table.

"No," replied Wang Kum briefly.

"Not any at all? How very strange!" And Mrs. Pennypoker looked questioningly at Wang Kum, who returned her gaze with impenetrable composure. "I thought I should surely hear from brother Nathaniel to-day. What can have become of the letter!"

"Wang no sabe," answered the Chinaman with an almost imperceptible shrug.

He turned away to go to the kitchen; but, just as he passed the window where Louise stood looking out, he contrived to let a fork slip from the plate in his hand. Louise started at the clatter, and glanced over her shoulder, to be met by a wink and smirk of infinite cunning, before the man stooped to pick up the fork, and finally vanished into the outer room. A moment later she followed him.

"Did you want to speak to me, Wang?" she asked, trying in vain to appear unusually dignified, as she faced the man who stood chuckling before her.

But Wang, by no means abashed by her manner, bestowed upon her a second wink of exceeding craftiness, while he slowly drew a note out from the loose sleeve of his shapeless blue coat.

"Wang mus' a forgot him; you no tell," he said softly, with a stealthy glance at the dining-room door behind him, as if expecting to see Mrs. Pennypoker appear on the threshold and swoop down upon him at any moment.

Louise glanced at the letter in her hand. She was annoyed to feel her color come, as she saw that it was addressed to her in Dr. Brownlee's well-known writing.

"Where did you get this, Wang?" she asked.

"Doc' Blownlee." And Wang Kum smiled knowingly.

"But he didn't tell you to give it to me this way, did he?" she asked again.

"He no tell; Wang sabe, all samee. Wang no fool." And Wang marched back to the dining-room, leaving Louise to read her note unobserved.

As she had supposed, it was merely a message to appoint the hour for a ride they had agreed upon for that afternoon. There was not the slightest reason that she should not have received and read it under the eye of Mrs. Pennypoker; but long experience had taught her that the ways of Wang Kum were past finding out, so she only tucked the note into her belt and went on her way, resolving, however, to warn the doctor to select another Cupid, in the future, to be the bearer of his messages.

Some weeks had slipped away since Ned's illness, and spring had once more come to Blue Creek. The crisis of the fever once passed, the boy had quickly rallied, and, thanks to the devoted care of Louise and the doctor, his recovery had been sure and steady, until at length he was pronounced nearly well enough to resume his former place among his friends. Then came the time of thoroughly disinfecting and airing the house, for Dr. Brownlee was not the man to leave any uncertainty as to results. His quarantine had been as strict as his later measures were energetic, and he had refused to rest until he was assured that no danger could come from his patient. Owing to the negligence of Dr. Hofer, the disease had been spreading across the creek, until the board of health had interfered, and summarily taken the cases from his care to give them into the hand of Dr. Brownlee, whose vigorous treatment had checked the trouble, even though it had incurred the hostility of the parents of the fever-stricken children.

But at last the doctor had said that all danger at the Everetts' was over, and Grant had been allowed to come home once more. In spite of the good times he had been having with Howard and Charlie, in spite of the motherly welcome of Mrs. Burnam, the boy had been thoroughly homesick during the period of his banishment from home. It was the first time that he and his brother had ever been separated, and Ned was his hero and idol, as well as his constant companion. During the long days of waiting, when the fever was at its height, Grant had wandered disconsolately about the house, refusing to be comforted, and looking so pale and miserable as to be a mere shadow of his usual bright self, and to cause Mrs. Burnam many an hour of anxiety lest he, too, were about to be ill. Then came the sudden change for the better, and, for a day or two, Grant was like a wild creature in the exuberance of his joy; but he was restless and anxious to be at home with his brother again, sure that no one else could take as good care of him as he. He had even waylaid the doctor on the street one morning, and tried to bribe him to allow a return home; but Dr. Brownlee was firm, and Grant had been forced to bide his time.

The whole Everett household had been radiant with its new happiness, during these last few weeks. It would have been enough for them all to have Ned brought back to life, after their terrible hours of suspense; and for days they hovered about the boy, almost unable to believe that their bright, affectionate, impish Ned was to remain with them, after all. Even Mrs. Pennypoker had cast aside her strict principles of discipline, and coddled him and fussed over him to her heart's content, while Wang openly prided himself on being the means of his recovery.

"Wang went 'way off out doors," he had confided to Louise; "all lonee; hollered heap loud to Up-in-Sky. Up-in-Sky no say anything; he sabe, all samee; came down heap quick to help Mas' Ned."

In the midst of this rejoicing there had come a cause for even increased happiness. On the morning after Ned had turned the dangerous corner, and started on his slow journey back into life once more, Dr. Brownlee had gone into the parlor where Mr. Everett sat writing letters, and had closed the door behind him. His stay was only a short one; then Mr. Everett came out, and went in search of Louise.

"Come, my girl," he said gently; "Winthrop is waiting for you. Your mother would have been very happy to-day, as happy as I am." And he led her to the parlor door; then he went away, and left them alone together.

To Louise, it had seemed as if the world had suddenly been created anew that spring. The days flew by like one long, happy dream, while she spent hour after hour amusing her brother during his tedious convalescence, or left him to Mrs. Pennypoker's care when she escaped to the parlor, to enjoy the doctor's short, but frequent calls. Ned had been as rapturous as his sister when the good news was told to him; and he had saluted the doctor as Brother Brownlee upon the occasion of his next visit.

"It's just too jolly," he had said, with the first return of his old, irrepressible manner. "I'd rather have you take Lou than anybody else I know; and I'm no end glad I helped it on. You know you'd never have come to the point, if I hadn't scared you both out of your senses; but"--he paused, and then asked wickedly, "but I say, Lou, what do you suppose the Reverend Gabriel will have to say about it?"

The Reverend Gabriel, in the mean time, had kept himself informed on the subject of Ned's illness, and although he had held himself at a prudent distance from all danger of infection, he had not neglected the young invalid. As soon as it was definitely known that the boy was on the way to recovery, Dr. Hornblower had sent him, through the safe medium of the post-office, a little book of "Sick-room Meditations," whose black cover bore the cheering design of a tomb under a pair of weeping willows. Though the gift was doubtless intended in all kindness, it was received with more amusement than gratitude, and Ned kept it under his pillow to read aloud choice bits from it, whenever Louise and Dr. Brownlee were together in his room.

But, during the weeks that the Reverend Gabriel had been unable to call at the Everetts'; he had been slowly making up his mind upon a matter of weighty importance; and now at length the time had come for him to carry out his intentions.

The Reverend Gabriel Hornblower, it should be stated, was a romantic soul; and, in his tanned, weather-beaten old body, there throbbed a heart as ardent as ever beat in the breast of a boy of eighteen. Its manifestations, however, were often a little eccentric, for its owner was as ignorant and unworldly as a child. For years he had fed his elderly imagination upon the most impassioned love scenes to be found in the pages of novel or biography. Unfortunately for him, there was nothing in the least modern about his literary taste; but he had confined his reading to the histories of the Evelinas and Cherubinas of yore, until his idea of the tender passion was as old-fashioned and stilted as the books from which it had been derived. Nevertheless, the Reverend Gabriel was becoming weary of boarding-house existence, and beginning to long for the comforts of home and the charms of conjugal society.

It would be hard to say whether the sight of Louise Everett's blonde beauty, or the contemplation of his own frayed cuffs and ragged buttonholes had been the moving cause; but the result was the same. Upon this particular afternoon, he had spent an hour in reading over one of his old favorites; then, seizing his hat and cane, with an air of desperate resolution, he had hurried out of the house, and up the street towards the Everetts'.

He was ushered into the parlor by Wang Kum, who assured him that Louise would soon be at home, and rolled out the great leather-covered chair from its accustomed corner, in order that the Reverend Gabriel might be as comfortable as possible, while he awaited her coming. Then he withdrew, leaving the guest to his meditations.

They were not altogether enjoyable ones, however. Wang Kum had told him that Louise was riding with Dr. Brownlee, and the Reverend Gabriel, with the jealous eye of a lover, was not slow to discern a possible rival in the handsome young man, who had been a constant attendant at the house, during the past few weeks. Moreover, the room was very warm, and the Reverend Gabriel was beginning to grow a little uncomfortable, for Wang Kum, with the keen malice of his race, had carefully arranged the chair directly opposite the register, which brought the heat from the stove in the next room. Dr. Hornblower had been feeling rather nervous, all that day; now he feared that he was becoming feverish. He drew his hand across his moist brow, and sighed anxiously. Could it be that he was going to be ill?

At length Louise came in. She looked so bright and pretty in her dark habit, and with her golden hair loosened by the wind and curling about her face, that the Reverend Gabriel felt his admiration momentarily increasing, while he gazed at her. And yet, something in her fresh, girlish beauty made him long to draw back from his coming interview, as he rose to greet her, and caught sight of his own dull, brown face in the mirror above her head.

"I hope I haven't kept you waiting too long," Louise said courteously, while she unbuttoned her gloves and slowly drew them off. "It is such a glorious day that we stayed out a little longer than we meant to."

"It is a fine day, a very fine one," returned the Reverend Gabriel, eagerly catching at the safe topic of the weather.

"Yes, and we were shut in so long that I enjoy being out, more than ever," said Louise, while she speculated vainly as to the doctor's motive for this call.

"You have had a painful experience," he answered gloomily; "a trying and painful experience; but I trust that you are benefited by it. My thoughts were continually with you during the--um--the ordeal."

"Thank you, Dr. Hornblower," Louise returned gratefully. "Our friends were all very kind."

"Doubtless they were," responded Dr. Hornblower, as he sympathetically wiped his eyes. "We were all grieving over the prospective demise of a young brother. And yet some consolation would have reached you, Miss Everett; love is the only pocket-handkerchief to wipe the mourner's eyes."

Louise blushed hotly at the reference. Although she had made no secret of the matter of her engagement, still she was a little surprised to have the Reverend Gabriel allude to it in such an unexpected fashion. But she was determined to carry off her embarrassment as easily as possible, so she smiled brightly, as she said,--

"Then you have come to congratulate me; thank"--

"Pardon me!" interrupted Dr. Hornblower, as stiffly as if his rheumatism had suddenly penetrated from his joints to his manners. "It is not yet the time for congratulation; and, when the hour comes, it is I who will receive them."

"You?" And Louise stared at the Reverend Gabriel in unfeigned astonishment.

"At least, so it is to be hoped," returned the doctor gravely.

For a moment, there was an awkward pause, while Louise wondered whether the worthy minister had suddenly taken leave of his senses, and the doctor writhed uneasily in his chair, as he realized that his hour had come. The hush was beginning to be painful, and Louise was just opening her lips to speak, to say something, no matter what, when she was suddenly struck speechless by seeing the Reverend Gabriel lay his hat and cane on the floor beside his chair, then clumsily kneel down before her and clasp his hands. For one brief instant, she supposed that he was about to give her the benefit of his professional services, and she composed her face to listen with befitting gravity; but his first words dispelled the illusion.

"Louisa," he began, in a tone so devoid of expression as to suggest the possibility of his having written out the words and committed them to memory; "Louisa, behold me a suppliant before you, begging, imploring"--

But Louise had started from her chair, and stood facing him, her cheeks white with mortification for herself and pity for him.

"Dr. Hornblower," she begged hastily; "get up, please! You mustn't say any more."

"But you do not catch my full meaning," he went on. "I ask you"--

"Get up at once," she repeated. "You mustn't say it; it's impossible! Suppose some one should come in. Oh, do get up!"

Yielding to her evident alarm, he awkwardly scrambled to his feet, and threw himself down in in his chair once more, with a force that pushed it back against the opposite wall.

"Truly, I never thought of such a thing," Louise said penitently. "I always supposed that you came to see Cousin Euphemia, not me; or I might have prevented this."

"Why should you, Louisa?" returned the Reverend Gabriel, with a cheerful assurance that grated upon her ears. "I am willing to wait and hope; my heart is eternally yours."

"Oh, I hope not!" she answered quickly. "Really, Dr. Hornblower, it never can be, never could have been; I never even thought of such an idea. You have always been very kind to me, I know," she went on hesitatingly, trying to soften her words a little; "but I thought it was only because you felt a fatherly interest in me."

"I'm not so old as you seem to think," began Dr. Hornblower testily; then, bethinking himself that this was not according to his models, he made a dramatic pause, before he asked his final question, "Is there, then, Another?"

Louise hung her head and blushed.

"I'm afraid there is," she faltered.

"And his name?"

The girl looked at him haughtily; then her face softened, as she thought of the mortification that she was inflicting upon the old man before her, and she answered gently,--

"It is Dr. Brownlee."

Once more the Reverend Gabriel hesitated. He had carefully rehearsed his part, until he was thoroughly familiar with it; but his imaginary interviews had taken only the one form, and he had never counted upon such an ending as this. However, he was resolved to carry it through to the close; and, after a hasty review of the ways of rejected lovers, he recalled the case of the luckless Alphonso Ludovico, and felt himself prepared to meet the new emergency.

"It is the end," he said slowly. "Pardon my intrusion, Miss Everett; I will no longer impose upon your kindness. I go forth upon my lonely way."

He started to rise from his chair, but came to a sudden pause, while a sound of rending and cracking broke the silence that had followed his tragic words. All unconsciously, Wang Kum had given him the sticky chair; and the heat of the room and the doctor's feverish agitation, had combined to produce the catastrophe. The Reverend Gabriel Hornblower was trapped as effectually as a fly in a pool of molasses, and could only struggle helplessly in his efforts to free himself.

Louise came to his relief, and together they succeeded in separating his coat from the chair-back, and he took his ignominious departure. The young girl stood looking after him, until he disappeared around the corner, then she fled to her own room, and into the very depths of her closet, to smother the sound of her hysterical laughter. But when at last she grew quiet, her face became very gentle once more, as she said to herself, in a tone of womanly pity,--

"Poor old man! But at least, I can keep his secret; not even Winthrop shall ever know."

In the mean time, the Reverend Gabriel had slowly betaken himself to his lonely room, where he laid aside his hat, and approached the mirror.

"No," he said to himself, as he stood gazing at the reflected face before him; "it wouldn't do; it wouldn't do. She's too beautiful; and I'm--too old." And he seated himself in his worn old easy-chair, and took up the book he had laid aside an hour before.

CHAPTER XVIII.

UNDER ORDERS.

It was less than two weeks after the Reverend Gabriel's call upon Louise, that Mr. Burnam came up from his office, one noon, with a letter in his hand.

"Well, daught," he called, as Allie ran out to meet him; "where's mamma? I have some news for her."

"News! What is it? Nothing very bad, I hope," she answered, as she seized his hand in both of hers, and hurried him towards the house.

"That depends," he said laughing. "Wait till we get into the house, and then I'll tell you."

"I don't believe it's much of anything," she declared scornfully. "If 'twas, you never could wait to tell us."

"We'll see about it," responded her father, as he entered the house.

But it was not until they were all seated about the lunch table that he would tell them his news. From the central office of the railway by which he had been employed for the past five years, a letter had come to him, that very morning, offering him the position of consulting engineer for the company, an advance which would bring him much honor and more salary. For a few moments there was a babel of congratulation and rejoicing; then Mrs. Burnam put an end to it all by asking quietly,--

"And when shall we have to leave here?"

"Leave?" And Allie turned to stare at her mother in consternation.

"Yes; of course we shall have to go away from Blue Creek very soon," answered her mother cheerfully; for, though at heart she was as sorry as Allie to leave her pleasant friends in the little camp, she was unwilling to let her one regret throw a shadow over her husband's happiness in his promotion.

"Leave Blue Creek, and the Everetts, and Marjorie, and all? Let's not go," urged Howard. "The old road isn't worth it, papa."

Mr. Burnam laughed.

"I'm sorry you don't think so, Howard," he answered; "but I'm afraid we must go. St. Paul isn't a bad place to live in; and we should have had to leave here this spring, anyway, for my present survey won't take me much longer. I'm to report for duty in two months," he added, turning to his wife once more. "Will that give you time to get ready?"

"Two weeks would do," she said promptly; "I haven't been your wife all these years for nothing. I'm sorry to go away from here, of course, for we've made pleasant friends; but I sha'n't be sorry to have a settled home. Besides, it's time the children were in some good school, if they're ever going to college."

"What do you think about it all, Charlie?" asked his uncle. "You haven't told us, yet."

"I'm about as much mixed up as Auntie is," he replied slowly, while he gave Allie's hand a consoling pinch, as it lay on the table, toying with her fork. "I don't want to leave the doctor, and the boys, and all, and this place has been immense fun; but, as long as I can be with you people, I don't mind much else, and, if we go to St. Paul, I can stay with you till I'm ready for college,--that is, if you'll keep me."

"We won't send you off just yet," returned his uncle. "Howard and Allie would have something to say about that, I fancy. Let me see; this is May, and I have to be ready by the first of July. We shall have to leave here the last week in June, so you must make the most of your time till then."

"Oh, dear!" sighed Allie, as she and the boys were starting for the Everetts', that afternoon, to tell the great news. "We never stayed so long in one place before, and I began to hope we'd live here always. We've had such good times, too, 'specially since Charlie came; and I don't want to leave all these people."

"'T isn't all of them, though," responded Howard. "There aren't so many I care about, if we could take the Everetts and Fishers and Dr. Brownlee along with us."

"And the mountains, and Wang Kum, and our ponies," added Allie. "Janey says she'll go too. But it's no use to try to count up what we're leaving, or I shall just sit down and begin to cry."

"Better not," advised Howard practically; "it's no end dusty, and we can't spend time to brush you off. Besides, St. Paul is right on the way to everywhere, and we shall see people when they go East. Don't you go to being in the dumps, sis; 't won't mend matters to grumble, and we've moved before without its killing us."

But in spite of his advice to his sister, Howard was the most disconsolate member of the party, as they sat on the Everetts' front steps, talking of the separation in store for them.

"It's a perfect shame," lamented Marjorie, who had joined them there. "You belong to us, and oughtn't to go away. I had it all planned out, too. We were all going to grow up here together, and have ever so much fun. Allie and I would keep old maid's hall, and have you four boys board with us. Howard would be a civil engineer, and Charlie a doctor, and Grant have a store, and Ned be a minister; and we'd just have an elegant time."

"'Specially me!" remarked Ned, in a tone of supreme disgust. "I've no desire to step into Dr. Hornblower's shoes, when the old man finally gives up and goes over the range. Preaching isn't in my line; I'll help Charlie keep his apothecary shop, and sell patent medicines. But, honestly, with half of us gone, the rest will be dismally lonesome. We shall need Allie to keep us straight, and Howard to keep us stirred up."

"And Charlie for general all-overishness," added Marjorie. "Say, Howard, do you remember the day we put Vic into the empty barrel, and turned a bushel basket over him, 'cause he would follow us, every step we took?"

Howard chuckled at the recollection.

"Yes. How he did yell! But do you remember the time we shut Marjorie up in the office closet, Ned, and then went off and forgot her?"

"That must have been before I came," said Charlie. "How did she get out?"

"What a question! didn't you ever hear Marjorie squeal?" asked Grant scornfully. "But, I say, you lads, do you remember that day that Charlie Mac came, and we"--Grant paused abruptly.

"We what?" demanded Charlie.

"Oh, nothing." And Grant retired behind Marjorie, to blush unseen.

"What was it?" urged Charlie again. "Go on and tell, Grant."

"You hush up!" And Ned gave his brother a threatening glance.

"I'm going to tell, then, if you won't," said Allie laughing. "If we don't, Charlie will think it's something ever so much worse that 't is. All was, the boys didn't mean to like you anyway, and didn't want you to come. The day you came, they went down to the station, and hid around, waiting to get a look at you, to see what you were like. And the worst of it all was"--Allie paused mischievously, and then went on; "they found you weren't half so bad as they supposed you were going to be."

"If we could only go back again, and start there all over fresh!" sighed Marjorie.

"We couldn't have a bit better time than we have had," returned Charlie. "We've made the most of our chance, and we may as well be thankful for it. Oh, but didn't I feel shaky, that first morning, when the train stopped, and I had to get out! Allie looked about ten feet high and thirty years old, when I saw her standing on the platform; and I was sure I was going to be afraid of her. Wasn't, though," he concluded, giving her hair a friendly tweak.

"Besides, 't isn't quite so bad as if we had to go right away," added Allie hopefully, as they rose to go home. "We have two months more; and there's time for ever so much to happen, between now and then."

But the two months hurried past them, and, before any one realized it, the Burnams were on the eve of their departure. As Marjorie had said when the subject was first mentioned, it was harder to stay than to go, for those left behind had to keep on in the same old routine, where they so keenly felt the loss of their friends who, on their side, were full of anticipations for the new places they would see, the new acquaintances they would make, while the bustle and excitement of packing kept them too busy to realize all that they were leaving behind them.

It had been decided that the Burnams were to go away from Blue Creek the last week in June, and, soon after this plan was arranged, Louise and Dr. Brownlee had announced their intention of being married on the twenty-fourth, in order that their friends might be present at the wedding, so the last few weeks had found the Everett household in as great excitement as were the Burnams. It was to be only a quiet church wedding, followed by a small reception. Louise had reduced Allie and Marjorie to a state of speechless delight, by asking them to be her bridesmaids; while the doctor had laughingly protested that Charlie and Ned should act as ushers, since they had been instrumental in bringing himself and Louise together. After a little discussion, this plan had been adopted, and the four young people were much impressed with their consequence, in taking part, for the first time, in so important a ceremony.

On the evening before the wedding, they all walked up together from their rehearsal in the chapel, and stopped for a little while on the Everetts' front steps, where they were joined by Howard and Grant.

"To-morrow, and the next day, and the next, and then it will all be over," said Marjorie pensively.

"I honestly haven't had time to think about it, this last week," said Allie. "We've been so topsyturvy and busy that I haven't thought of anything but packing and the wedding."

"No; we'll be the ones to do the thinking," said Ned, as he stretched himself out at his ease, on the railing to the little porch. "With Lou married, and you three going, there's nothing else left for us to do. I'm going to turn hermit, and move up the gulch."

"I wouldn't, before fall, if I were in your place," returned Howard, in a tone too low to catch the ears of the others.

"What's next fall?" asked Ned listlessly.

"Don't you give it away that I told you," said Howard, while he joined his friend on the rail; "but I happened to hear your father talking to my father, to-day; and it's all settled that you and Grant are coming to St. Paul, next winter, to board with us, and go to school. Hush up!" he added, as Ned gave a little exclamation of delight. "Don't tell the others, for I oughtn't to have said anything about it; but I couldn't hold in any longer."

For an hour more, they sat there; then Grant's voice broke the hush, as he put his head in at the open window of the parlor, where his sister and Dr. Brownlee were sitting in the moonlight.

"That's the seventh time you've said good night, Lou," he remarked, in a hollow tone; "and I should think the eighth 'most ought to do the business, unless you want to be dead sleepy, to-morrow night, while you're in the middle of being tied up."

The next evening found the chapel crowded. Every seat was occupied, and the side aisles were filled with the miners and their wives, who stood waiting to look on at the marriage of "our Miss Lou," for she was a favorite with them all.

At length the murmur of voices died away, as Mr. Nelson took his place in the chancel, while the little organ pealed out the opening strains of the wedding march. A moment later, the doors swung open and the bridal party entered, Charlie and Ned leading the way, with Allie and Marjorie following them, while Mr. Everett and his daughter came after them. Louise was beautiful, in her simple white silk gown, although she looked a little pale and nervous, as she saw so many eyes turned upon her. Then she forgot it all, all the crowd and the excitement, and even the friends gathered about her, and her face grew radiant with her love, for Dr. Brownlee had met her at the head of the aisle, to lead her forward to the altar; and above the low notes of the organ, she heard the quiet, earnest voice, as it followed Mr. Nelson's through the familiar words,--

"I, Winthrop, take thee, Louise, to my wedded wife."

Their troths were plighted, the ring was slipped into place, and the blessing was pronounced. Then, as Winthrop Brownlee and his bride turned to face the congregation once more, the organ rang out in a triumphal march, and the bell in the little tower overhead burst into a merry peal. The sound rolled far up and down the valley, and the mountains echoed back the happy tidings; then the evening quiet once more descended upon Blue Creek Cañon.

L'ENVOI.

The last leaf ended, ere you lay My book aside, and turn to rest, Read here, old friends, between the lines, My loving memories of your West.

The distance shortens to my eyes; To-morrow's sun will sink to rest Behind your hills. One day is all That separates us, East and West.

Then hasten forth, my little book, Speed on your way, nor pause to rest; But, turning towards the setting sun, My greetings bear from East to West.

"TREMONT," Twenty-seventh May, 1892.

THE END

www.ingramcontent.com/pod-product-compliance
Lightning Source LLC
Chambersburg PA
CBHW060518290526
45791CB00001B/438